Table Of Contents

My name is Keaton Grant, and I can honestly say that I have filled every role possible on a basketball team. I have journeyed from sitting on the bench, to being a defensive player, all the way to becoming a leading scorer in several games. I have even played the calm and decisive leader, and let's not forget hitting a few big shots throughout the duration of this career journey.

Have you ever had full access to behind the scenes of a top-ranking Big Ten team? Or had the luxury of experiencing a program on the rise, whose quest is a national championship? Well if not, here it is. You have officially been GRANTed access to the Purdue Boilermakers' basketball team's 2009-2010 season. Our basketball team has climbed many mountains, faced a multitude of adversity and personal hardships, yet still we proved our ability to accomplish feats even when doubted by others. Coaches of all levels who aspire to be more amendable will find a safe haven within these pages. They will gain the intuition to read and every one of their players, both on the court and also in their personal lives. This is the true test of an effective coach. Can he put aside his pride in winning to mentor a player in a way that will catapult him to true success? Advice will range from how players can improve in areas where they may already be gifted to how to prepare potential players who wish to play Division I basketball, and finally, the inner workings of a top-ranked basketball team. As for the athlete, this could also be a good read to help you through the bouts of adversity throughout your own careers. This book is also for basketball fans that wish to see what only the players and coaches have access to. I will now offer you a chance to walk in the footsteps of those who have lived it. You will read about the downtime and random laughter in the locker room as well as the extreme intensity on the court.

By Robbie Hummel

As I was growing up, I always wanted to know what was going on behind the scenes of a major college basketball program. I loved Valparaiso University as a kid. Bryce Drew was leading them to a sweet 16, and I couldn't get enough of the Crusaders. I can't even tell you how much I would have enjoyed a book written by a player on that team as a 4th grader in Valparaiso, Indiana. There is a lot more to college basketball than meets the eye. The countless hours of practice, weight training, conditioning, and team interactions that fans never get to see are lost in only our memories. That's why, in my opinion, Access GRANTed is great for not only Purdue fans, but for college basketball fans in general. We had a special group of guys for the 2009-2010 season. It was a season of ups and downs, but I think every one of our fans that watched us would say that we always played hard, and we always competed with class. Those two things that categorized our team basically characterize Keaton Grant. He has fought through adversity, just as our team did, but always learned from his mistakes. He didn't let the trouble he found his sophomore year, the surgery before his junior year, or his struggle to consistently shoot the ball his senior year get him down. Keaton always worked on his game. He also always played his heart out. That's something that as a teammate you can really respect and appreciate about another guy. There were times in games where I thought Keaton may pass out from being so tired, but he played through it. KG also always treated everyone on our team with respect. I know that if you asked everyone of the guys on our team about Keaton, it would be nothing but positive responses. He has a great sense of humor and is awesome to be around. By the time of his senior year, he had grown into a father figure that gave advice to the younger guys in the locker room. In the end, essentially winning the Big Ten regular season championship for us, hitting back-to-back crucial shots in Minnesota rewarded him.

During the season, I saw Keaton taking notes in a little notebook during a road trip when we were rooming together. I didn't think much of it, but when he told me that he had written a book about the season it all started to click. I am honored to write this foreword for KG, as he was a great teammate, but more importantly he was a close friend. I hope all Purdue fans read this book and can look back on what a great year we had together. With great wins over West Virginia, Tennessee, Ohio State, and Michigan State, I know I'll never forget those games. Enjoy the memories that Keaton brings back. I know I did, and I hope you do too.

Chapter 1

Preparation

The preparation began with the loss to the University of Connecticut in the Sweet Sixteen competition during the 2009 season. I did not feel that we were satisfied with merely making it to the Sweet Sixteen; we had prepared ourselves for that stage the year before, when we lost to Xavier, to make it to the Sweet Sixteen. Some teams feel content when they make it to the Sweet Sixteen because it was their top goal. We wanted more. In the 2009 season, we were still undeveloped and unprepared to play at the level needed for advancement to the Elite Eight.

I still remember the moments after the UCONN game in the tournament of the '08-09 season. In the locker room, there was a still silence. There was an atmosphere of hunger; to get back to the tournament and compete for a national championship. We decided that from that moment on, each time we huddled together for our team chant, we would chant "Final Four" because that was our ultimate goal.

In my mind, as I was thinking about the season that just passed, I knew that we were at least going to return to the Sweet Sixteen the following year and, most likely, advance beyond that. I knew we had primed ourselves to be better than the past season, and we would work even more avidly to accomplish the goals that we set. We knew, in 2009, that we could have advanced farther in the tournament than what was predicted, but we did not do so. *Why?* I asked myself; we were athletic, we were talented, we were skilled and we played pretty good defense. But that night, we played *through* our offense, which is something that was not the bread and butter for us.

So, what does it mean to play *through* our offense? It is simple. In the Big Ten, most teams are known for their aggressive defense. They depend on their defense to win games. That was also true of our 2008-2009 defense; it was *our* bread and butter. Looking back at our preparation for the tournament, we had prepared out of our ordinary set up. The criticism for losing the game against UCONN goes to the players; that night to win the game, we needed to excel in areas where we performed best, which was defense. At that point, we needed to rely on what was best for the team in order to gain that win. Individually, we needed to do what was required of each of us for our team to be successful. That is one thing we lacked that night, and the price was a loss to UCONN. We had strengths, and we did not utilize them. Defense was and is our bread and butter, and we neglected it, which resulted in our season ending much earlier than we anticipated.

When gearing up for the next season, it is crucial that you are honest with yourself and analyze what your strengths and weaknesses are and how you can improve in them. In my head, I felt like my junior year was a disappointing year in comparison to my sophomore year; from a statistical standpoint, almost every number was cut in half.

One misfortune you cannot always prepare yourself for is an injury. My injury did not happen in an instant; it happened over time. Time was my enemy. Concrete was my enemy. You might wonder, why concrete? What does concrete have to do with the game of basketball? If you live in colder climates, most likely you have played basketball indoors on a wooden, knee- friendly surface. Being from Florida, I played the majority of my games outside on rock hard concrete. My knee paid the price. Tendonitis became unbearable. I had surgery after my sophomore year on the patellar tendon of my left knee, and was unable to do anything at 100% for six months, making it even more difficult to stay in shape for shooting and ball handling for the upcoming season.

What followed for the entire season was that I was unable to get into a rhythm. I was playing catch up. It was as if my mind knew what needed to happen, but my body was not in sync with my mind. I felt one step slower than my teammates. I felt as if I had aged. I felt like I had lost my edge. My teammates, even nicknamed me "Old Man." But old men are wise with insight; I'm about to bestow my wisdom.

Time would come into play again, before my senior year. This time, immediately after my junior season, I only took three days off from working out; I was determined to take my game to the next level. Most athletes take up to a month off after the season. For me, a month off would have included too many distractions. I am a Florida native. I am lucky to see my family once or twice a year, at the most. In the past, that time off had typically been spent returning home for a visit. But a visit home would lead to other distractions besides family; friends felt entitled to my time also.

Old Man Wisdom #1

Other distractions (and I am sure I am not alone here) are the bits of advice you get from people when you go home. Everyone wants to be your "friend" and get on your good side by telling you how "good" you were last season. They go on with how your coach "should have done this and that" or how you "need to such and such," placing doubt in your mind and disturbing your mindset. My advice is to avoid these people; run in the opposite direction. These people only want a piece of you. What I mean by a "piece of you," is that they want to control you. It empowers them to think they can have that kind of influence on you. They name drop you to their friends.

It makes them feel better about their status in life, but it accomplishes nothing for you. Not only will that throw you off your game (because you will start to believe what they say), but it could also make you an un-coachable player, and one thing which is bad for a team is an un-coachable player. Un-coachable means you develop a stubbornness. You are not willing to do what is best for the team because of your own selfishness and interest in individual gains. Here's my confession: I know this because that was me at one point in my career. Listening to negative talk from "friends," I thought that the coaches had it out for me. I was not willing to accept the coaching that they were trying to give me.

I wanted to take my mind off all that and sacrifice for something greater that would benefit me in the long run, and quite frankly, I felt like I did not deserve a break, so I went to work right away. I had ambitions in mind that I wanted to accomplish my senior year; I wanted to leave my senior year with a bang. This led to my tough decision to stay in Lafayette, by myself, to work out with no distractions. I became introspective and made a list of what needed to be fixed or improved to build me into a better player and enhance my team as well.

My handwritten list:

```
☆ Ball handling
    Finishing
    dribble Pull-ups
    A floater

    improve 3pt Shooting
    shots off Curl cuts


☆ Lock Down Defender
    Lower My T.O.
```

You might ask, just what goes into preparation? The preparation, for me, begins with staying in shape. This is a feat I have always battled throughout my college career. I was determined to eliminate it as a factor in my last season. I consulted with my former AAU coach, Tom Toppings, who coaches Nike Team Florida out of Clearwater, Florida. Over the phone, I relayed what I considered to be my strengths and weaknesses. He was well aware of them because he had watched several of our games on national television. Together, we created a workout plan. It included the number of days per week that I would work out and the time per session. Next is the mental preparation for the regimen and the academic portion of my stay on campus in May. At Purdue, they call it Maymester. I was enrolled in a manufacturing class that I was NOT looking forward to taking. But, as it turned out, the instructor, who was an actual employee of a manufacturing plant, was extremely insightful. Class was almost three hours a day and Mr. Savage did an excellent job teaching us about the success of making sure systems work properly and people enjoy their work. Along with the vast amount of technical information, there were also life lessons for the working person.

With Maymester off to a start, I began the commute in the afternoons to Indianapolis for workouts at St. Vincent's, where Ralph Reiff is the director. My basketball workouts were with Ed Schilling. Now I thought I had worked hard prior to these programs, but working out with those two men took me to a whole new level. The first time I worked out with Ed Schilling, I almost died. After the first 30 minutes of the workout, I was hunched over, feeling light-headed, but I stayed cognizant of the benefits of what I was enduring. I truly do not think my mind nor my body was prepared for the workouts that he was afflicting me with; what I was experiencing was tougher than a game, so I knew that when the game came around, the challenge would be so much easier to overcome. When playing two games back to back, the body and mind must be prepared. When going through the preparation, everything is mental, and whatever you tell your mind to do, the body will follow. If you have the ability to teach and train yourself to be a strong-minded person, then the sky is the limit. I persevered through the workouts regardless of how tough they were. I have never quit one thing in my life and I was not going to start. I embraced the challenge to prepare my game; I got motivated and upgraded my workouts to six days a week at St. Vincent's for a month straight. It got a little costly commuting back and forth from Purdue to Zionsville, where coach Schilling did his workout, and then to St. Vincent's which was a couple of exits further down the road.

Purdue is also known for its reputation of running a clean program. With six days a week of driving back and forth to and from Indy, 120 miles round trip, I was forced to gas up my car three times a week. At $45 per fill-up, it cost close to $150...per week! It is against NCAA policy for the basketball program to give their players money to accommodate their personal trips. The first two weeks of Maymester and Indy drives/workouts flew by, and I still felt like the workouts were not enough for me to see improvement in my game. I kept telling myself, every day; that there is no limit to what I could do. I grew dissatisfied with my progress, and don't get me wrong, my progress was not being limited by my help in Indy. I just wanted to see immediate improvement and was growing impatient. The staff in Indy was doing everything right; I was just not advancing forward as fast as I wanted. So, I got in contact with Coach David Woods, a former graduate assistant at Purdue University and the current West Lafayette High School basketball coach. I asked him if I could go to the high school Monday, Wednesday, and Fridays to use their basketball gun. Purdue, surprisingly, did not have a basketball gun, but the high school had this equipment available. A basketball gun is placed under the basket and passes you shots from a firing tube. It goes at a faster pace and can take the place of someone rebounding. Coach Wood was more than willing to oblige because he knew I wanted to improve my game.

The high school is only a couple of blocks from campus and their gym is air-conditioned. Mackey Arena is looking forward to air conditioning with its remodeling due for completion in 2011. This is not a criticism to Purdue, but having an accessible climate-controlled facility will be advantageous. The advantage of having a practice facility with the renovation in the Mackey project will be that a player would be able to go to the gym and work on his game anytime without having to worry about finding someone to turn on the lights or someone to help unlock the closet where the basketballs are stored, which is what players have to do until the project is complete. Other schools have this advantage now. The players can go to their gyms 24/7 and 365 days a year to work on their individual game because they do not have the limitations that Purdue has. Competitive facilities are something that I would highly consider if I were assisting my son or daughter with choosing a college with an athletic program.

In June, the entire team was back at Purdue for summer workouts in the weight room, youth basketball camps, summer school and open gym. Open gym is something we all anticipate, (minus the heat on Keady Court), because it is casual and loose. It is the perfect time to bond with each other and work out any small personality issues that always arise within teams. It's also when we get to meet and form relationships with the incoming freshmen. Open gym gives us that sense of team chemistry that prepares us for the upcoming season. Chemistry is so vital among a team, even if most team members are veterans. The slightest changes and adjustments can throw a team out of sync. It is also a time for establishing new leadership for the upcoming season. So, open gym is enjoyable but critical to the program.

With everyone back from their breaks, we discussed what we did throughout May. JaJuan Johnson was one of the players who worked out with me at St. Vincent's. He was also invited to the Amar'e Stoudamire Camp in Phoenix. E'twaun Moore was back from Paul Pierce's camp and Rob Hummel, who was with the USA team playing in Serbia, had not gotten back yet. JaJuan, frustrated because he also tried out for the USA team and did not make it, told me he was going to use the disappointment as motivation this summer. He wanted to show Bo Ryan, the University of Wisconsin's head coach, that he made a mistake by not keeping JaJuan as one of the "big men" on the team.

It felt good to have most everyone back; *I* was especially glad because it can be quite boring not having a friendly face from the team around just to talk to or shoot the breeze. Plus, I missed the camaraderie. Looking at the team as a whole, you could sense that we had more swagger; we were better prepared, both mentally and physically, than the year before. During open gym, a lot of time turns into one-on-one sessions between two men who want to show the rest of their teammates how they have improved their game. There were ten of us out there, but it often turned into one-on-one games between two men who wanted to showcase their progress so the rest of us knew they were *ready to play*. This was the place to prove to your teammates the upgrades you have made to your individual game.

So we were at the point where we had been playing open gym for two weeks; with our improvements and teamwork, we resembled an All-Star celebrity team!

Old Man Wisdom #2

I went so far as to tell everyone after one open gym that it "looks like we really have become celebrities," as everyone's little bumps or bruises immediately sent some people to the athletic trainer, Jeff Stein. They looked forward to leaving practice or open gym just to avoid what they felt was either too difficult for them or too tedious. They had no qualms with leaving the gym, as if they felt they did not need to work through the pain to get better; they were *satisfied and content. This is what I mean when I say we were playing like celebrities. I told them, "We cannot be satisfied with just making the Sweet Sixteen like last year. We need to go past that and strive for excellence. We aren't going to just make our goal to be Big Ten Champs, like we used to start out every season. We are going to go above and beyond striving to just make the Big Dance. With those minimal goals in mind, we used to stay in and fight through the little bumps and bruises. We were not simply satisfied with our game and with just making the stage but now, when we have higher goals, like reaching the Final Four, like playing in our own backyard at Lucas Oil, **now we start playing like celebrities**? When there is an injury that occurs doing the season and you might not be 100%, you can fight through the pain knowing that he team is counting on you to do your job. The team needs to be assured that you are going*

23

to step up when you're needed the most; to making that play all the way to making a last second shot; to making a critical stop on defense; to get us to the Final Four. None of us are ready for this celebrity nonsense, and more importantly, the team cannot afford it!"

Chapter 2

Preseason

On the first day of class, there was something different about that day. I was reflective: It was my last first day of college. Who would have ever thought that I would be in this position? Not that this would be the last day of my knowledge gain; it was going to be my last first day of education allowing me to play collegiate basketball. Up to that point, to be quite honest, I hated school. I really did not like any aspect of school, except the girls. For most, girls are probably the biggest distraction in school besides the drugs, alcohol and partying. But one thing that always kept me level-headed enough to stay on top of my academics was basketball. I was not going to let something I deemed as insignificant as school, in my mind, keep me from playing basketball.

Old Man Wisdom #3

But you always have to keep your mind on the bigger picture. Hindsight is 20-20; I now realize how much school has helped me and how essential to have a degree. An education is something that no one can take away from you. Furthermore, knowledge is a valuable asset that you can always use to your advantage and for the advantage of those who are close to you. Originally, college was a means to an end; for basketball. In retrospect, I know that an education, unlike basketball, is a guarantee. Basketball can be taken away by injury, time, economy or competition. Your education, however, is yours to keep, yours to grow and yours to share. Share with those who can benefit from your knowledge. Share with those who can benefit from your mistakes. Share with those who can benefit from your experiences.

The night before the first day of fall classes, we had a team meeting. We were given our Big Ten Tournament Championship rings. It was the first prize hardware I had ever received. It felt so great to have a ring; it is the feeling that reaffirms the reason you play. After the rings were awarded, we were in awe at just how elaborate they were; diamonds, lots of metal, our names, our school name, they were exceedingly generous in size. It gave us all an inkling of how it would feel to win national championship rings. I vowed to myself, right then and there, that I wanted at least two more rings; another Big Ten ring and a national championship ring. I waned to conquer this feat with the team gathered around me at that moment in our locker room. I felt that it would be nothing short of a fairytale come true. *We* could do it.

We had our first day of individual workouts during the first week we returned for fall classes. I was anxious to show the coaches how much I had worked on my game; I was bringing a lot more to the team: ball handling, pull-up jump shot, endurance and leadership. There were freshmen in my workouts; they did pretty well for their first workout under the circumstances of being newbies. It was tough trying to keep up with everything that was thrown at you on the first day of workouts. It brought memories of my very first workout as a freshman. We were in the Purdue Co-Rec.; hot as hell, slippery floor, and when you are a freshman you are just trying to do what you can without making any mistakes. I remember Coach Cuonzo Martin, who is now the head coach at Missouri State, was running our workouts. We had a mixture of everything, offense and defense, and I remember with about twenty minutes left in the workout, being on one knee huffing and puffing, gasping for air, feeling light-headed like I couldn't go on. My body had never been pushed to that limit before. I remember Coach Martin kept saying, "Do you want to quit!?" In my head, I was saying, "Hell yes, do you see me over here about to pass out!?" Then he said, "Whatever you tell your mind to do, the body will follow." I had never heard that proverb before that moment. I told myself that I was not going to quit, because I had never quit anything in my life. I may not have turned heads that day in the freshman workouts, but I do know I showed them that I had heart and I was not a quitter.

Being around so many different players throughout the years, I have seen many instances of people quitting, both on themselves and their teammates, to failing out of school. There are so many excuses for quitting. The two main reasons people give up are because they either cannot handle the pressure or they do not believe in themselves. There are so many people around the world who could have become big time college players, but they quit on themselves. Unfortunately, they are back in their hometowns doing the same things that they were doing at the time they left; nothing changed for them.

Old Man Wisdom #4

*Never let **anyone** tell **you** that you cannot do something! I think that is the story of my life and why I have never been a quitter. There have been plenty of times when coaches, administrators, principals and teachers told me that I would not amount to anything, just so they could destroy my confidence and elevate their own egos. **But** if **you** believe in **yourself,** you do not need anyone else. I was a firm believer in God and myself, and I owe my prosperity on the court and in life to those strong beliefs.*

So, on that first day of conditioning, I was a senior, so I shouldn't have been the one who was nervous about the first day. We have a tradition on the first day; there is always a timed mile run. The guards have to finish within five minutes and thirty seconds and the big men have to finish within six minutes. There were two exceptions on that first day for Rob and JaJuan, who were two of the *big* men. Rob had to finish in five minutes and ten seconds and JaJuan in five minutes and twenty seconds. I hadn't run the mile in two years because of the surgery on my left knee, so it was like being a freshman all over again and there was never *any* charity given on mile day. During my freshman year, I finished the first day mile in five minutes and thirty-one seconds. That was not one of my better days. They made me do it over the next day. I did it in five minutes and twenty-eight seconds.

For my senior year run, my goal was to stay with E'twaun, Mark Wohlford and Ryne Smith. I knew I could use them as guides to make sure that I finished in the allotted time. We took off and everything was going according to my plan until the transition from the end of the second lap to the start of the third. That is when I started to question myself, "Am I going to make it?" My legs became tight and I started seeing stars, but I kept telling myself, "Just stay with them, stay with them." It always goes back to your body following whatever you tell your mind to do. We had one lap to go when Coach Painter yells, "You got to go, you got to go!!" A sense of panic set in, "Oh Lord, I am not going to make it!" When he said that, I thought "Dang, it's too early for me to try to kick out the last bit of energy." Coach said, "Everyone behind Stevie (Loveless) needs to pick it up!" I looked up and, of course, I was *behind* Stevie by 30 yards. Worry began to set in at that point. E'twaun, Ryne and John Hart took off; it looked like they were in fifth gear and I was in third, just barely picking up my legs. They created a distance between us to the point where I was wondering, "Wow, how am I going to catch them?" People have said when they are running long distances, it feels like a monkey has jumped on their backs and they cannot move. There was no monkey, it was a *gorilla!* And he held a hammer in his hand going to work on my lower back because it was as tight as a young kid holding on to his parent for dear life in the deep end of a pool. I was using all my strength to stay within close range of my teammates. I just closed my eyes and kept running until I heard during the last 110 yards that the time was 4:55! All I remember thinking was "THANK YOU GOD I MADE IT!" I finished the mile in five-twenty four. In fact, for the first time ever, we all made our times on a first day of conditioning! Was this a sign that the upcoming year would be extraordinarily special? (In all my four years of being at Purdue, and for as long as the coaches said they had been timing mile, there had never been a whole team to complete it the first time.)

We were approaching the last two weeks of pre-practice conditioning, and after that is when the real business would begin; it would be time for practice. It is a funny thing because conditioning is supposed to prepare an athlete for practice and get him in shape enough to step right up; but not at Purdue. Our practices were so intense from the very beginning that no amount of preparation could help our bodies get ready. We did running and drills so much in practice that conditioning helped us to just participate until we could catch that second wind. The first week of practice was *ALL* defense and there was no exception. We would rarely touch on offense in the first week of practice.

During the last two weeks of conditioning, we ran sprints on the court. Every year we always had a freshman or newcomer who would go down and couldn't make it. On the court, sprints might have been easier for someone like me because it is all just sprints, but it is tough for the big men due to the changing of direction. At the start of on-the-court conditioning, someone always broke down and cried because they lacked the stamina.

It was the last week of conditioning, which was always the worse by far: Four days straight of conditioning. Each progressive day of conditioning on the court the expected times of the sprints were lowered. Typically, the big guys were the ones who missed their times in the sprints, but this year, the guards would miss them too, because our recovery time was shortened and we had to complete a full court sprint each time. During these sprints, the big men sometimes felt as if they were receiving double the conditioning, because once you missed your time you had to make that up with another sprint. Usually people started missing them around the fifth repetition, but some were starting to miss it around the second one, which was most likely a lack of effort.

Old Man Wisdom #5

Remember, you are only as good as your weakest link. So no matter how much some teammates feel sorry for themselves, you cannot let them miss their time, you need to have their back and push them. You need to help them break through the wall they are trying to climb.

So at the end of conditioning, a big man had to run some of sprints again because of the times that he missed. Standing there watching, we were powerless because we knew he wanted to give up, but we could not run them for him. He was struggling. Finally, on the last make-up sprint, the coaches showed a little compassion and upped his time. While we were waiting, we decided that one of us should run with him, to show him we were behind him; that we were a team and would not leave a teammate behind. On the last rerun, he started strong and was on a good pace. But then it happened; he slowly but surely started to give up again. He did not believe that he could do it and started to give in to the pain. He stumbled and fell on his face, like a sniper had shot him in the back from a thousand yards out. He did not finish the sprints nor was he able to do his individual workout for that day.

Chapter 3

Satisfaction and Achievement: What it takes.

As a senior, I pondered where I would be after my senior year: in the NBA, overseas, or even playing basketball at all? A day did not pass when I did not think about how I was going to play during the season. Both questions replayed in my mind over and over. My excitement for the season was due to how far we predicted we would go. I felt that this *had* to be the year for something special. I *truly* felt like we could make it to the Final Four.

Old Man Wisdom #6

Our primary concern must be the team and not individual things. I think back to other seasons when we had different seniors and different mindsets. Some of the upperclassmen who were on the team at that time were plagued with individual mindsets; something that can be difficult to overcome because one may feel like he has already invested a lot of time and personal sacrifice for the team. He may be puffed up because he feels it is his year to show and prove what he can do. This is all so true, but you don't want your personal goals to be more important than the team.

Senior year, in itself, can be a distraction. It is your last year in college. You start thinking about partying more and getting that last hoorah of your collegiate career. Your mind is thinking, "Man, there will never be as many women to choose from as I have here, right now, in this relaxed setting!" You think about how you may not have this opportunity once you leave the college life. This is how most people think, but I have always tried to view things from a different mindset. I made a decision to be a lot *less* social my senior year. I had the rest of my life to go out and party. I only had one senior year to play basketball. Which was more important? It was an easy decision.

Success and achievement are my motivation, and I dedicated my senior year to focus on basketball, but it makes me think back, looking at other sports teams. I have noticed, after a loss, a team will go out to party and act like there is not a care in the world. Clearly, they did not lose the game on purpose, but it is imperative to have enough teammates who care about winning; teammates who are not satisfied to just say, "Well, we *almost* won." Almost won does not hang banners, and almost won does not get you rings, especially not in NCAA Division I competition. A winner will have a mindset that says, "I am going out to perform to my maximum ability, and we are taking no prisoners."

As a team, we could not be complacent with just being in the NCAA tournament; you cannot be satisfied with just being in a close game with a top-notch team. One thing that comes with success is the experience in how to win games. That is the difference in the highly-ranked teams and the not so highly-ranked teams.

It was September 25th, the day before we were to play Notre Dame in football; it is one of the things that I would miss about college, the fun of watching and supporting fellow athletes in their competitions. We usually had open gym on the mornings of football games, but this week, we had open gym on Friday before the game. So it's Friday, and people just wanted to relax after a long, exhausting week. But we rarely played open gym on Friday, so it should have always been something that people enjoyed: good solid games. Some teammates kept asking, "When are we going to "stack it up?" (This was when we were about to wrap up a session and go into our chant.) But they were already asking this after the first couple of games. That irritated my focus as a competitor. Why? We rarely had opportunities to just play for the enjoyment of it, and we should have been thirsty to go against each other, simply to make each other better.

After that game finished and the complaining began, I put on my senior leadership hat. I brought the team together. I said, "We need to get our priorities straight because certain people want to "stack it up" just because it is a Friday. Granted, it's been a long week, but not going past *half* court on defense? Come on!" What's worse was that the people who were complaining were those who had little or no playing time. "You should be itching to show that you want playing time and that you will not back down." I told the guys that we "break it down" (same thing as stack it up) *after* each workout, conditioning, and open gym. We had to earn the right to chant "Final Four." If we got the privilege to chant this, it would be only because we conducted ourselves like a Final Four team. "Doing all this complaining is not a winning mentality, we need to be the hungriest team in the nation, and everyone needs to be held accountable for what they bring to the court."

Playing defense, that is what we did at Purdue; that was the staple of our program. After that little talk, open gym was more competitive; you could feel the atmosphere change, to want to get better. The dangerous thing with having to take a time-out is you can't wait for the action to be stopped and discussed before the team wakes up, you cannot have an on and off switch in a game; doing such things will get you defeated.

Chapter 4

Start of the Journey

The first day of official practice had finally arrived. Man, oh man, it was a good day to be alive! This day was a new beginning on a journey to something great. However, this October 17th could have also been the longest practice ever, especially for an upperclassman. It was a long three hours. I had endured it so many times and I snickered to myself as I observed the freshmen. There they were, all dressed early, pacing back and forth with excitement, like little kids squirming the night before Christmas to open presents. Before practice started, I talked with some of the upperclassmen, who too were glad to be going to practice; Rob was so relieved to be healthy, like me, again. E'twaun, who usually had this laid-back look before practices, was excited too, because I noticed he actually had his shirt all tucked in and was on the court extra early, a lot earlier than usual.

This was a bit of a surprise; there was not so much yelling and frustration from the coaches. I think it was because we had so many returning players that they knew that we would get it right, the drills, the plays, the rebounding, the defense and the enthusiasm. Practices were running along smoothly.

A week before our first exhibition game, we had a scrimmage against ourselves with referees. This was so Coach Painter could discover different sets of people who played well together. As soon as the scrimmage began, it was downhill for me; I was out of control, going a hundred miles per hour and looked like an eighth grade player. I had about ten turnovers *and I missed* plenty of easy layups. I was *supposed* to make people look better, being the point guard. That definitely did not happen this particular day. Also, my defense was less than mediocre; it was the worst I had ever played since I started playing in the scrimmages. The worst part was that my pride of being a senior was shattered. I was no different than the nervous freshmen. So much for being all smug about their anxiety on the first day. I suppose I didn't know myself so well after all.

The preseason banquet was a different experience for me that year and rightfully so. This would be my last one. Dan Heman, of Heman Lawson and Hawks, CPA has sponsored the banquet since I entered the program as a freshman and it went from being held at the Purdue Union to the University Inn. On that particular night, it was so crowded that there was hardly any room to pull your chair out, because it was sure to bump into the guy behind you. The tables were so full that you had to keep your elbows in, too. The whole room was buzzing. As I was squeezing to get into my chair, I just let my mind wander. I was thinking, *I am actually a senior*. It had been a long journey, but the time rapidly flew by. This was my last season as a Boilermaker. It was all encompassed in hearing the Mackey crowd get so loud that it gives you goose bumps and you cannot hear yourself think; hearing the boo's and "you suck," and having everyone against you except those who walked out of the locker room by your side while you're on the road in the Big Ten. Just the excitement of being out there playing at the highest level and on the biggest stage is something that I will cherish for the rest of my life.

My mind comes back to the banquet. That night, we heard speeches from the different members of our coaching staff up to the president of Purdue. During the event, a different coach discussed each player in their assigned graduation class. They noted their improvements and what they were looking for from each guy for the upcoming season; showcasing each individual and promoting him to the alumni and boosters in the room. The banquet is almost like a roast in a sense, as they crack jokes about the players and reveal some of their comedic sides. I laughed along with everyone else in the room, when Coach Rick Ray started in on Lewis with the endless vertical challenges that he will always face because of his stature. Everyone was having a good time. Chris Kramer's parents were in attendance. Mark Wohlford's parents were there. My heart ached because I knew mine would have attended if they had been able.

Old Man Wisdom #7

Speaking of parents, I want mine to know just how proud I have been to have them. They have quiet wisdom and a quiet gentleness about them, too. I will always revere my parents. They worked hard and still are to this day, in order for my brother and me to have better lives. They have their principles and they are simple. We know where we come from and what is expected of us as citizens. Respect for God, family, friends or any human being. Always give the person the benefit of the doubt. Never jump to conclusions. These are just a few of the lessons I have learned. I will always, always value my parents.

Once the preseason concluded, and all the preparation as a team and as individuals ended, it was time for action; all the training and conditioning that we endure would now be evaluated, as a whole, to see just how intensely we worked.

Chapter 5

Start of the season

With the start of the season right around the corner, another situation arose. Kelsey Barlow became a little worrisome about whether or not he would be redshirted. He pulled me aside and asked if I had heard. I told him no, because I honestly hadn't been informed one way or the other; it was actually coming as a shock to me. My advice to him was to encourage the coaches to think twice about it; you have the two preseason games to show to them that they do not need to redshirt you, so play hard and prove what you can do.

You might wonder why redshirting can be viewed negatively by a basketball player. It can be difficult for a player, although it has its pros and cons. I have witnessed players use that redshirt year to get better as individuals. The player can work on his shooting and the different kinds of weaknesses that his individual game may lack. On the contrary, there is the possibility of picking up bad habits during that year, too. I have seen some redshirted players become un-coachable. "It's not like I am going to play tomorrow. I don't have to play hard because I'm not getting any minutes." This negative outlook of the red shirt jumps into their psyche and it mentally defeats them. They lose sight of the reality that the next season will be here before they know it. I know from having several friends who are football players that redshirting can actually be an opportunity; their bodies have time to mature and grow to take the pounding that a typical football player takes and it also gives them extra time to complete their degrees.

With Kelsey, I tried to suggest that he envision himself out on the court. I suggested that he stay to his game while focusing on how he can change the coaches' minds. I said, "Just play your game and play hard within your physical limits and everything will take care of itself. If you really want to impress them, just do three simple things: play defense, play hard and rebound." He said, "Okay, then that is what I'll do." I asked him how he found out about the potential red shirt. He said that one of his friends went on his *Facebook* page and put it up as a joke; from there, it was on the website of *Gold and Black*, and finally, it made the sports news in the Purdue *Exponent*.

Old Man Wisdom #8

I explained to Kelsey how imperative it is to be careful to whom he discloses his information; you never know who can hurt you even if their intentions were not to hurt you. Some people think that may be pulling a harmless joke, and they mean no harm. With the numerous social networking sites out there today, you have to be EXTREMELY careful about what you post and who you send it to. It only takes seconds to either trash someone or create a rumor that could be devastating to you or your teammates. Just use your head. In public, people have cell phones that they can use to upload unflattering pictures of you that could also embarrass your teammates.

Before each game, regardless if it was home or away, we stayed in a hotel and the coaches confiscated our cell phones. They did this to ensure that we received the right amount of rest to be ready for game time. One particular night before a game, some of us, mostly with dark skin, were chilling in our room. (I do not ever want to come off as sounding like a separatist but for some reason or another, usually this group chilled together. Don't get me wrong, we were all very close and we had a lot of light-hearted banter that went back and forth about our particular skin color.) Anyway, Bubba Day was a regular who stopped in to chill with us, and others might show up too. They would walk in the room and talk about 'integrating" with us. This was a joke among some very close teammates. In fun, we would turn around and say something sarcastic about them being in their white clique.

On this particular night, we had a special guest, Rob, which was rare. We started to talk about how it felt to be in the position that we were in as a team; how there were very high expectations and how much of a buzz there was around school surrounding us with the student body. We also discussed what type of crazy things people would say to us in class and how sometimes, the fans might know little things about the team that we thought the public wouldn't know. It was exciting to see the fans who were interested and in tune with us as a team; that showed true love. We also discussed how it could be fun when we traveled to different places and experienced different arenas that we might have never dreamed of seeing. We also talked about the great years of recognition from the fans and community. It made the journey even more worthwhile when we got love from the fans at different functions around Purdue, and how enjoyable it was just meeting new people and seeing how excited the community was for each season to start.

Also with what the future could hold for us all, if we had a good year, we would experience opportunities to place at the next level because that had always been a dream of ours. Then, we started discussing how practices sometimes dragged along. I'm sure all teams have had these same types of discussions. One thing about Coach Painter is that, he would rather be overly prepared than miss one thing. I'm sure any coach in America feels the same way; it is their job. Their families' well being is at stake and they want to do their best. They probably feel like they do not receive enough time in preparing their teams for the season. We also talked about how we had to rely on each other for advice on and off the court, and I think that is one fact that brought us even closer together.

We were discussing what we see as we look at different teams and their coaches around America. We, for example, could see a coach rip a hole in one of his players, and jump in his face within a matter of inches, but the player intently listens to what the coach preaches to him. The player would not take it personally; he would go out and do what was just asked of him. A prime example of this is Michigan State and Coach Izzo; we were just amazed how his players looked to him as a father figure. This was apparent by the way he got into his players' faces, and how they took heed to his words and put their arms around him to show him love.

You might be wondering why I am discussing the different coaching styles and player-coach chemistries. My teammates and I were left with somewhat of a void when Coach Cuonzo Martin departed for Missouri State. Coach Martin was our Coach Izzo. He was our liaison with the head coach. He was a confidante. This is not a criticism about the current coaches, but it is a fact that when Coach Martin left, he took with him that person who exemplified being personable. It is not that we do not respect the new coaches or the demeanor of Coach Painter. We just miss that person whom we had grown to know over time, who conveyed a level of comfort when we needed advice. Time will be the factor that will tell who will fill those shoes for Purdue, but it will be hard to replace Coach Martin's warm communication style; the way he motivated and pushed us to be better was almost equivalent to him being on the team playing the game right along with us.

Chapter 6

Lewis: Never Saw This Coming!

The first official game was moments away, but we would not be at full force because Lewis was out with an injury. It happened during the practice before the game following his two-game suspension. He was so ready and excited to play. The practice before a game is always like a regular practice, with not really much being held back. We were going through drills at full speed, with all contact, but this practice quickly changed the face of the team. During a full court drill, Lewis went up for a layup against Chris Kramer; Kramer landed on his foot. We were playing hard and it could happen to anyone, but the thing that Lewis kept wondering was why were we going so hard on a full-court drill a day before a game? We found out that Lewis needed surgery and there was a great chance that he would miss the year. It was difficult to see something like this happen because he worked so hard to get himself ready for the season, and it happened right before he played his first game.

Lewis is someone who was an important piece to the team. He started twenty plus games last year; he possessed a great deal of experience that made our team even deeper and more versatile because of what he brought to the table on defense. The news soared that Kelsey (Barlow) would not be redshirted; most likely because of what happened with Lewis. We were going to need everyone in the guard position.

After Lewis got the word that he needed surgery, he told me that he would be back. I said, "What do you mean?" He said, "There is a chance that I can be back in January or February. I want to play again with you KG and play for a national championship; I do not want to miss this moment." That was the reason why he was thinking about not taking the redshirt year.

Old Man Wisdom #9

That is definitely a man's decision. My advice to him was he had to do what is best for him and his family; to sit down and talk to them and not depend on the emotions of the moment. Lewis was a very strong person and a fierce competitor; he had been through many tumultuous times. I marked my words; Lewis would be back. He had a huge heart, a heart of a lion. I had no doubt that Lewis would be back playing ahead of schedule.

The first game was against California State Northridge. We were ranked seventh, which meant nothing really. They (CSN) were not concerned with the ranking; their goal was to come in and knock us off at home and take no one lightly. We were one of the few teams in the nation who on their first official game were playing someone who went to the NCAA tournament the previous year. Everyone was energized; you could feel it in the atmosphere around campus. This is what everyone had been anticipating. This was what the Paint Crew, especially, had been waiting for as they were camping out the night before for season tickets.

Chapter 7

Paradise Jam

On November 18th, we traveled to the Virgin Islands. I was comparing it to the other places that I have been throughout my career, and no offense to the Virgin Islands, but Maui, Hawaii was by far, the best place I had ever visited. It was like a dream to see the clear blue water and experience the amazement of snorkeling. It was the most incredible place I had traveled and played thus far; these amazing places were just some of the best benefits of playing college basketball. When we arrived, it transformed immediately to a business trip. The first game was against South Dakota State. We won the game, but it was a very ugly one. It was a sloppy game for us; we did not play to our full competence and Coach Paint let us hear it, too. He told us that the game we played was embarrassing; he was not satisfied just because we won. He warned us that if we showed up like that for the rest of the tournament, we would not win it. Not only was Coach Paint upset with the team as a whole, the other coaches were disgusted too.

One thing I learned in four years was how coaches were never satisfied; they were very demanding, as they should be. They wanted us to meet our maximum aptitude. If you were in the locker room after the game, you would have thought we lost, but that is how it is when you are aiming for perfection. With all that was said that night and looking around the locker room at the facial expressions of the team, I would hate to be Saint Joseph's, our opponent the following day. We prided ourselves on defense, and that did not happen. South Dakota State had thirty-seven points in the first half, despite our goal to keep every team under twenty five. I can't even remember a time prior to that when a team had thirty-seven on us in the first half. We knew that when we were to play Saint Joseph's, it was going to be a headache for them…

I was right; we *did* come to the game. We had the mindset that we would beat them by fifty. They wouldn't come close to their hope of having a chance of winning the game. We would hang our hat on defense; the point guard alone turned the ball over eight times. The defense that night was just smothering; there was no breathing room for them. At Purdue, that is one thing that a basketball player will learn, and that is how to play defense and play hard and do it to the max. We forced Saint Joseph's to turn the ball over twenty three times! And we beat them by twenty-eight. Hey, if there was someone who knew my team, it was me. That is what we strived to do to every team, making it extremely difficult for teams to get into their offense.

The next game was against Tennessee and we had been waiting for this match-up. Tarrance Crump, an alumni player and a close friend of mine, had been talking to Tyler Smith, the starting guard for them. I played against him in prep school and my freshman year when he was at Iowa, so I was familiar with his game; I knew a couple of other players on the team also. We were ranked as the one seed of the tournament; they were two. ESPN predicted us losing to them; adding more fuel to our fire; we loved it. Tarrance and Tyler had been talking a lot about this game; of how Tyler was going to do this and that and how we didn't have a chance. I told him to tell Tyler that we were no slackers and not to think for a second that they were going to win.

We were at our pre-game shoot-around and Tennessee came on after us. Tyler was one of the first ones to walk in the gym. I guess he wanted to do the staring game; as if it was going to intimidate us. We were the wrong team to try that on; I thought it was humorous. Consequently, we were also staying in the same hotel, so there had been a big buzz leading up to this match up; stares in the hotel lobby. It was going to be an intense game. This is why you play the games; this is what makes it all worthwhile, playing ranked teams on TV for a championship tournament trophy... how sweet it can be.

Tip off goes up and they jump on us pretty quickly. Even Tyler had a dunk over Kramer that got the crowd hyped in the first minute. We knew that their defense wasn't nearly as strong as what they were showing us, so we just needed to settle down; we would be fine. The game went back and forth in scoring, pretty much for the entire game. It had come down to what we continually worked on in practice. The score was 73 to 72; we were ahead by one; we just needed *one* stop. Wayne Chism had the ball at the top of the key and he tried a three-point shot to win the game. But as soon as he shot it, he knew it was off, because he chased after it immediately. We made a successful stop. E'twaun got the tournament MVP, and Rob made the all-tournament team.

Back at the hotel, we watched the highlights and it was a little strange because the commentators spoke as if *we* had lost, like we somehow got lucky that we beat Tennessee. We were used to it but we wondered what it would take to get the respect from them; it didn't come easy. As E'twaun, JaJuan, Chris and I were on the elevator with Coach Paint's wife and daughters, a Tennessee freshman was in the elevator with us. E'twaun made a comment about some people who just got off the elevator, nothing disrespectful, but the Tennessee freshman just had this angry look in his eye like he wanted to do something. I told him, "Don't try anything crazy," and as he was getting off, he asked what I had said, and I repeated it so that my words were not mistaken. We did not want anything to get started when there was a family in the area. No one got hurt or offended.

Old Man Wisdom #10

You need to respect those around you in any situation, especially when there are children present.

Our freshmen came to the room and said that some other players tried to jump them from the bushes, but someone came along and they gave up. But the night was not over. There were even more surprises. We all decided to go to the managers' room to play the Wii and chill a little. But there was a situation with another opposing player that night on another team, one who didn't even play. We didn't pursue the issue because we realized that we had a lot more to lose than they did. Wow, so much for good sportsmanship. But we were on cloud nine; we won the tournament. We were just going to enjoy our night and the glory of winning a tournament. People dream of one day being in the position we were in and just knowing the enormity of what we were to experience brought smiles to our faces.

Chapter 8

Me, Still Struggling

Old Man Wisdom #11

I still haven't been able to get on track shooting wise and this is when things can become dangerous as a player; you have to stay focused; but not just concentrate on yourself, which is easier, said than done. You want to do well for yourself, of course, and you are going to be a little selfish at times, but you also have to play within the system.

That was one thing that I did not do; I tried to be overly aggressive at times and took poor shots, so when the Wake Forest game came around, I did not perform well, and my family had come to the game to watch. I wanted to play well because they rarely get to seem my games in person. I stayed awake the whole night after the game.

Even though we won, it still didn't sit well with me. I was happy that we won, but I wanted to do well individually. I didn't get one bit of sleep that night. All I could hear was my clock on the wall, the hands ticking, like it was symbolic to *my* time, like it was telling me that time was getting short, like I needed to seize the moment and get on track; like this is your senior year.

The frustration was starting to build because I could feel myself second guessing things while looking at film. It seemed that I was rushing my shots; I was just not comfortable with what I was doing. My attitude was that it was a coaching problem, but in reality, it was me and only me. The coaches were not out there playing; I was. Coach Paint was the type of coach, like any other one, who rewarded productivity; the one thing I had been failing to bring to the table. In my head, I didn't feel that way; I was wondering, *how come when I make one little mistake he is taking me out? How comes he always says that my shot is a bad one?*

I lay in bed one night at about five a.m. just thinking about throwing it all out the window and just going for mine, taking it upon myself to be more aggressive and see if I could get out of that funk. I needed to be me and not worry about passing the ball as much as everyone else thought I should. But then I remembered how everyone had a role on the team. My role was not to score; that's how it seemed to be conveyed to me, at least. I said to myself, "I'm just going to be more selfish and more aggressive and see where it goes." My gut told me that when *I* scored more, we were even more successful as a team. This was one of the longest nights I'd had at Purdue; this is how much my performance on the court was affecting me. I needed to clear it all out and just play like I was capable of playing.

The next day, I definitely put up some extra shots before practice while trying to catch a rhythm before the next game. This was our first road game and it was against Alabama. They were a talented team with a new coach, so their ultimate goal was to knock off a top ten team on their home court. Before the game started, a fan, who was drunk, tried to talk a little trash to us. These funny incidences are a reminder; when we were on the road, the one thing that we would continue to hear, no matter where we went or what we watched on TV, is that we were overrated.

While we were warming up, the fans made signs that were probably the most creative that I have seen. They had downloaded a picture of one of the freshman off of *Facebook*. It showed him in a cowboy outfit and the sign said, "Brokeback Boiler." We tried not to laugh or retort back to the fans; if we did, we would be giving them attention, which is *exactly* what they wanted. They also had a sign with a picture of one of us in a Buzz Lightyear costume, and it was even more amusing because none of *us* had ever seen those pictures on *Facebook*.

We came out strong, and they came back with a run of their own that put us in the hole early; we were down by 16 at halftime. JaJuan and I were in foul trouble in the second half. During the second half, we hit them with a Boilermaker special, and we came back and won. They were drained towards the end of the game; you could see it on their faces. We overpowered them on defense and outscored them by twenty-four in the second half. It was the best comeback win I have been a part of and it gave us even more confidence, since it was on the road. Someone had dared me that if Alabama won, I would have to put on my *Facebook* status that they were the best team in

America. I accepted it because that is the kind of confidence I had in my team's capability. I was willing to challenge anyone at anytime when it came to the team. I will be completely honest; I was slightly worried in the first half when I saw the score, but I knew somehow we would pull it out. This team was definitely comprised of a bunch of fighters and no quitters.

Finals week began, and I was going to use that time to get extra shots up and rest my legs at the same time. I was thinking of the team throughout that season and I noticed that the team was a lot closer than we were all the other years prior that I had been there. We did more things together as a team outside of Mackey. I think any team knows that the more you are around each other, the more it helps with team chemistry. It is interesting because even though we improved by doing things as a team, we still didn't "chill" with each other like other teams do. Sometimes we were a very segregated team, but still so close together; I had never been on a team with such an interesting dynamic.

What I mean by "segregated" is we had cliques that we hung out with and rarely socialized as a whole outside of basketball, unless it was an all-team function including the players and the coaches.

Old Man Wisdom #12

It is important to know each and every player in a relaxed social setting by going to parties and other events. Even with the segregation, we did gel so well together on the court; we didn't miss a beat. Sometimes we already knew what another teammate was going to do when we were on the floor together. That was the benefit of playing with the core players for so long. Many other teams don't have that because they will have a couple of players who attend college for one year and leave. For the most part, we were in it together. I'm not criticizing teams who have players who only go to college for a year and then leave for the NBA, but there is a benefit of building a program up through the strength and the unity as a team when you have guys who have been around each other for three plus years.

Chapter 9

Wooden Classic

The Wooden Classic was our next game. Rob and I were saying that this game was going to be an interesting game for us to play. Ball State starts the game, and they were being physical with us. This was something that we were expecting because *we* did the same thing to them the previous year. But that year was on their home court. This time it would be on Conseco's floor, where the Indiana Pacers play. Oddly we always seem to play well in NBA arenas. We were not going to take them lightly; the plan was to just go out and handle business. There were a lot of elbows being thrown and a lot of trash talking. The most surprising thing was that Rob got into the trash talking and that was one thing that he did not normally do. He and the Ball State guy were going at it while I was bringing the ball up. I could just hear them as they jogged behind me.

You know when you have potentially taken a team's confidence when they start arguing with you and arguing with their own teammates. The most satisfying thing, to a defense, is when the opponent's guards are arguing who is going to get to take the ball down the floor.

We have had opponents do that numerous times throughout my career because they wanted nothing to do with our pressure. But as the game was coming to an end, we were about to win. During that time, Coach Paint said if they throw a punch, we need to be ready for that and make sure we don't throw one back. JaJuan just smiled at me with a little smirk, and I knew that meant if someone threw a punch, we didn't know how much self-control we would actually have in the game. It is vital to have self-control during the game because the consequence of violence could be suspension. But that is the last thing on a person's mind in the heat of battle.

We won by close to thirty and we got the trophy. Our team was happy to win but it didn't feel like we fought for it; we were happy to receive a victory but it just was a different feeling, one that I have never felt before. Talking to the other players, they felt similarly. Even though it was a regular season game, it was different just because it was the John Wooden Classic. My freshman year, we lost it to Butler; that is the only loss that we have at the John Wooden Classic. My sophomore year, we played Louisville and I liked that game just because we got to play against

Coach Pitino's team. When coming into college, there were several coaches that I wanted to play against and Coach Pitino's team was one of them. During my junior year, we played against Davidson. That was definitely a fun game to be a part of because they had one of the leading scorers in the NCAA that year in Stephen Curry, who now plays for Golden State Warriors. We held him to less than fifteen points; he was not ready for the type of defensive attention that we showed him. I know that he was tired at the end of the game. I kept getting texts after the game that we were playing them so well that they changed their channel to another game, which is a good and bad thing. It was good because we were handling our business like we needed to. It was bad because that was a regional game and, of course, we liked to be on television just like anyone else.

Chapter 10

Close to End of Pre-Conference

One thing that JaJuan said to me in the weight room before the SIU-E (Southern Illinois University – Edwardsville) game was, *"KG, don't you want to eat?"* (This was a reference to whether or not I wanted to make a lot of money playing basketball.) *"Do you want to get a nine to five?"* It was a motivator and I told him we were going to get this done. Nothing was going to stand in the way of us achieving greatness.

The last home game before conference was against SIU-E and after the game, we would have three days off, which was unheard of at Purdue when it came to in-season breaks; that caught everyone by surprise. After Coach Paint made the announcement that we would have a three day break, he followed that with a warning; if we played like we are already on vacation, this would never happen again, I know it was tough for him to let us off for three days because Coach Paint is a worker.

It was game time; the lights were on and what do you know, we *didn't* play too well in the first half. It appeared that we weren't getting a three-day break after all.

But we definitely picked it up in the second half and I finally, I repeat, *finally* got some rhythm in my shooting and had a good night. We ended up winning by twenty-seven.

Coach Lusk and I were talking after the game and he told me that it was good that I persevered, and I told him that I just kept telling myself the *next* game would be the game for me to break through. That next game would be the one when I would shoot well.

Old Man Wisdom # 13

*When you are a shooter and you are playing, you always have to stay positive and **never** bring any negativity in your mind to give yourself any doubt about your game or question your shooting or your shots; let no one rattle your game or how you play.*

We were undefeated up to this point and we only had had one true road game (Alabama) and plenty of neutral sites. We wished that we could have truer road games; games that would give us a good challenge that would better prepare us for when we were going into Big Ten play. There are teams around the nation that are fortunate enough with their scheduling which allows them to play talented teams that are sure to be playing in the Big Dance. We took a major step in that direction by scheduling West Virginia. That game would be a home game, however, but they were still a tournament team. This was one of the most exciting and anticipated games since Duke, and you know that Coach Huggins had his boys hyped and ready to play, as you could have seen on the TV. He was a very intense coach.

I did not make plans to return home to Kissimmee, Florida for Christmas because I wasn't expecting to get a three-day break. Visiting home is a luxury when one chooses a school far way; something that the local players on the team did not have to consider. I think that is the one thing that was always very difficult to deal with, not being able to have my family come to games and just being away from their presence. The average player was only able to go back home, at the most, two or three times a year.

The biggest thing that helped me with being away from home was attending prep school in Maine for a year before I went to Purdue.

But during this particular Christmas break, Momma Grant blessed me with her presence; she came up and surprised me. She planned to stay with me for ten days. I got home-cooking quality time with my mom, one on one. It was the best present in itself. I couldn't have asked for anything more.

Mom and I started talking about the season and she asked me how I thought it was going thus far, I told her it was going well because we were winning. Regarding my personal season, I told her I was not even close to being happy with my performance because I had expected so much more from myself. She told me to pray and leave it all in God's hands; everything would work out. She had said one thing to me before I left for prep school. It has always stayed with me and she still says it to me:

Momma Grant Wisdom #1

"Everything happens for
a reason."

I took my mom's wisdom with me to deal with an upcoming game. She continued her heart-to-heart with me as she told me, *"You know that you have not been playing to your potential. It seems like you are waiting for something. You played better when you were hurt your sophomore year than when you were healthy."* And it made me think: If my mom can see that, then I know I have to do better. She said, *"You are healthy and have no excuse to not play like you are supposed to play."*

Chapter 11

Finally, Big 10

Our first Big Ten game was on the road against Iowa. Just like Purdue had experienced a slump before I arrived, Iowa was and had been in a similar situation for three years. Their spirit seemed like it left them for a while, even the fans showed us as much enthusiasm as their own players. No one wants to be in that situation, and it is always tough clawing back. But it will happen for them. There will be a turning point.

We started off the game a little shaky. Iowa was getting plenty of offensive rebounds in the beginning; something we have not been good at since I had been at Purdue. We made it extremely difficult for them to get into their offense with the pressure that we were giving them. They really only let Payne bring the ball up for them; he plays forty minutes and with our pressure, he was going to wear himself out before the game ended.

At halftime, we made our adjustments and came out strong. While I was pressuring Payne, I whispered in his ear that he was going to be tired as ever after the game, but that he only had twenty minutes and then he would be able to relax. We were able to get him to play at a speed where he was not comfortable. I saw him after the game, and he was being helped up from the bench by the trainer. He was cramping up and looked like he was sore. I sympathized with our opponents because the defensive pressure that we put on them was so tight and they were not accustomed to it.

We started the Big Ten season off right and with a victory; that was huge.

Old Man Wisdom #14

*When you are on a journey to do big things in the Big Ten, one thing that you must do is **win** on the road, which is a difficult thing in this league. You have to take advantage when you are on the road.*

Chapter 12

A Marquis Game

The game that everyone had circled on their calendar: West Virginia. Coach Huggins and the Mountaineers had come to town. They were ranked in the top ten. The game would be on ESPN and everyone would be tuning in. This one was going to have Mackey shaking because the Paint Crew and Purdue nation would be so loud. The game was sold out, and the Paint Crew students had already started to camp outside for the game so that they could get good seats. As with Coach Pitino, I had always wanted to play against Coach Huggins because he is a very intense coach and his players play rigorously for him. I did not know that he and Coach Paint were good friends, so this brought even more excitement to the game.

There was so much riding on this game making it one of the best games to watch thus far in that year. It was number four versus number six, and it would be a marquis win for us; it was going to make our tournament résumé look so good.

Old Man Wisdom #15

You need to have great wins against great teams when you are aiming for a number one seed in the tournament.

One thing about West Virginia is that they were big in every position. They started Da'Sean Butler at the point position and he was *6'7*. With that being said, I think that should have worked to our advantage because he would be forced to handle our pressure. We came out in the first five minutes and threw the first punch. They were turning the ball over, they couldn't get into their offense; they didn't know what hit them. We defeated them by 15 points. It was later relayed to us right after the game that Coach Huggins was anxious to practice the next day, because he wanted to see which one of them was going to quit first.

Chapter 13

Back in the Big Ten

We returned to Big Ten play and were home against Coach Smith and the Golden Gophers, a talented team. They were notorious for playing hard but inconsistently. You never knew what they would bring to the court when you faced them; a very talented unpredictable team can be very dangerous. As we were seated on the bench waiting for our names to be introduced for the starting five, Rob whispered to me that the crowd was disappointing. We had recently defeated the number six team in the nation and yet Mackey was not packed. Maybe it was because it was all taking place during the Purdue winter break. We loved our fans, but sometimes it was difficult to predict whether the stands would be packed or not. We were a top 10 team with many people forecasting our place in the Final Four, so Mackey should have been be sold out, no matter who we played. We were trying to do something exceptional, and we wanted the fans to be a part of it.

If we beat Minnesota we would tie for the record as having the best start to a season in Purdue basketball history. In the second half, we were up by seventeen. We always got into it with Minnesota; it never failed. When the game was almost at end, we figured that there was no way they could win. They still attempted to commit a cheap foul anyway. We began trash-talking back and forth; it was just the competitive nature in both our teams mixed with the intensity of both coaches. We were talking after the game, getting ready to go home, saying how we seemed sluggish and needed to pick it up. We didn't need any losses to teach us a lesson. Even though we won, we were still overshadowed in rebounding, something that hadn't happened in a long time, so we knew that we needed to improve our game.

85

86

Chapter 14

Tough Stretch

One of the toughest places to play in the Big Ten was the Kohl Center at Wisconsin. They had just lost to Michigan State before playing us, so we knew they would try to get the bad taste out their mouths and work hard to gain a win over us. Wisconsin was a tough team to play because they ran the swing offense. They were also similar to us in that they rarely lost on their home court. JaJuan was so eager for the game because Bo Ryan, the head coach for Wisconsin, was the head coach of the USA team that cut JaJuan in the summer. So he wanted to show Coach Ryan that he might have made a mistake, even though it was a committee decision. He told me he was going to be geared up for the game.

Fortunately, we won at their place two years in a row prior to this. We had to make sure that we rebounded because they always did such a good job at it. In the game, we guarded the swing as good as anyone could guard it, but when the shot clock began winding down; they had to make a one-on one-play. They completed them every time, or they would get an offensive rebound to have another shot at it. It was our first lost; we were not able to contain their guards. Jordon Taylor, a sophomore who came off the bench to replace Trevon Hughes, earned twenty three points. He was making play after play after play. It was just pitiful how bad we were on our one-on-one defense that night. It was our first lost but we watched the tape and went back to what we do best. The coaches made sure that we were ready for Ohio State at home, which was our next game.

Evan Turner had recovered and was back from his back injury, which had kept him out for a month. So, it was understandable if he was a little rusty from being out of the game for that long. The game was going well as Rob had an unconscious first half; he was dropping three-point shots one after another. Ohio State had no answer for that because they were sitting in a zone. Rob put twenty-nine points on the board in the first half alone! It was an even more extraordinary night for him because he had received his thousand-point ball before the game started.

In the second half we were ahead by fifteen points with eight minutes to go. Our opponents started pressing to keep us out of transition; it actually made us turn the ball over. Their press was usually just pressure enough to slow you down in transition. One thing that we hardly ever did was lose our composure, but we let it happen during that game; we lost our composure so badly that it cost us the game. I had a key turnover at the end of the game that was costly because it was an empty trip on offense. We had the ability to tie the game. Evan Turner must have benefited from his month long vacation because he earned thirty-two points! I suppose you could say we were part of the welcome back party; he had a field day. It was a shock that a strong team like ours, which had played in so many pressure-filled tough games, lost our composure the way we did. Our biggest problem was exposed again this game: *rebounding*.

Any time we lost two games back to back, it never failed that Coach Paint would come in early and put our roles on the white board, outlining what he wanted us to do and what was expected of us. JaJuan and I were discussing this while Coach Painter was writing the roles of each player on the board. We were asking each other, "Does it seem like they lose confidence in us when they reiterate our roles?" We lost two games and probably needed to have a sense of urgency. JaJuan and I were nervously bantering a little back and forth predicting how the coaches were going to approach us with the pressure. Some of the team would react like they were depressed, like the whole season was over. The board contained our areas for needing improvement and what things we were lacking. There was always a comment about defense because that was an area where we strived for excellence. But it could make us also feel like there was sense of panic; the coaches would enter practice like someone had stolen their whole bank account. We felt uneasy; we understood being upset from the game because we were too, but those games were over and all we could do was get better the next day. The coaches gave us the silent treatment and you could guarantee that there would be a lot of yelling and cursing in practice.

We could always tell what type of practice it was going to be by the body language of the coaches. The assistant coaches just seemed real tired because they had been up all night scouting for the next team and watching film; anytime that Coach Painter didn't say anything to anyone and always went about whistling loudly with no type of rhythm, then look out and make sure your shoes are tied tight and be ready for a tough practice.

John Hart and Ryne Smith had been practicing very well; Ryne had come a long way from not playing at all and getting spotted minutes. You could tell that he was a whole lot more confident and he had worked extremely hard in the off-season to put himself in that position. He was no longer interested in sitting on the bench and in the off-season, he did something about it. Ryne had worked on his game, although some of us on the team had thought that he was going to be redshirted his freshman year.

John was in a similar situation and he was redshirted his freshman year, but he had shown significant improvements throughout practices and was just ready for an opportunity to present itself. It was an interesting thing to see the two of them next year since Chris and I were graduating. They would be competing for the playing time we vacated. I thought they were both doing a good job of using their experiences to help themselves in the future, so I was glad to see them sticking with the program.

The practice before we were to play Northwestern, in spite of losing back to back games and in spite of the meeting that we had before practice where there was a lot of yelling and cursing, was, where the running and sending a message wasn't as bad as I thought it was going to be. In my fourth year of the program, I would have to say that I felt that coach understood how dragging us in the dirt with our tongues hanging out, knowing that we had a game in the next couple of days, was not effective when the quest was for a national championship.

Also in my four years there, the next opponent had not gotten any easier. The game against Northwestern should have required nothing more or nothing less than just pure concentration, patience, and discipline. We had lost to them the year before on *senior night,* which made it all the more important. Playing against Northwestern, it just went against the majority of our defensive principles. It went against taking away passing lanes, helping side defense and staying tight off screens. It was most difficult on our point guard because he had to jam their point guard full court; they do a lot of speed cut-offs during the first pass that our point guard makes. They usually took up all of the shot clock and it was rare for them to get an offensive rebound, so that means we were going to be on defense for another thirty-five seconds.

So this was a game that we needed to utilize to bounce back. Knowing our team, that is something that should have happened. This would be the only time that we will play Northwestern in conference. The game was at Northwestern and playing them always made us feel like we were back in high school because the gym is so small compared to the other schools in the Big Ten. It was also like a home game for us because of its close proximity to Purdue. In my time spent at Purdue, this was the first time the game was sold out. Also, we had Brad Miller in the stands this day. We wished more former players would come back to see the newer players who followed in their footsteps. I always wondered what things needed to happen to encourage past players to return. We heard about other teams whose alumni players returned to work out with the present players and share their knowledge with them. For example, Jason Williams would go back and help Nick Calathes at the University of Florida with his point guard skills or Nick would train with Jason in the summer, receiving tips on how he can improve. Last summer was the first time I had seen so many former players back in Mackey at the same time. Part of the reason they were there was to support the summer camp Carl Landry held at the West Lafayette High School. Carl, David Teague, Marcus Green, Tarrance Crump and Brandon McKnight were all in attendance. I know former players can be extremely busy with other obligations. I would like to make a more than conscious effort to create an even stronger bond between former players, the coaches and the present players; we could all build and form an elite player/coach brotherhood. With that being possible, I believe we need to all remember the past, present and future players and coaches in order to help each other improve as the Purdue basketball program grows.

Game time, baby! We came out ready to play. We were ready to end that losing streak, but that changed quickly. After they took the lead from us, they led the entire game. It was like we were having breakdown after breakdown on defensive assignments. We would guard their offense well and lock them up, but we could never finish with a rebound. Rebounding, our Achilles heel, kept rising to the surface, exposing us. I wondered what it might feel like to have a team beat us and then have the fans storm the court. I did not have to wonder any more. We ended up losing 42-23, the worst since the UCONN game.

We could sense that the fans were anticipating rushing the court; we could see that with only a minute left in the game. When their fans rushed the court and bumped us, we just wanted to release our frustration and punch one of them, laying them out right on the court, but it was very important for us to keep our composure and swallow the loss, because *we* lost the game, not our opponent.

When we got into the locker room, Coach wrote the number "328" on the board and circled it. He sat there for a second and just let us stare at that number. We had no clue what it meant. He said, "This is what their (Northwestern) ranking was two years ago in college basketball, the worst in the NCAA and they out-rebounded us by 19 points." That statement hit the heart with a dagger. That was the longest ride back to the school. We lost three in a row, which put us at two and three in the Big Ten conference; we dug ourselves a huge hole.

Many people were saying it couldn't be done, even some of our fans on their *Facebook* pages. They said that we would just have to try for another tournament title in the future. Those three losses just gave us more adversity to overcome. We were two and three in the Big Ten, which did not help our résumé for the tournament when we were striving to get a number one seed. With all of that being said, practice was sure to be a nightmare.

Practice was the hardest it had been all year; there was plenty of running and a whole lot of yelling. Anytime anyone made a mistake or missed an assignment on defense, he ran a suicide as penalty. If someone did not get a rebound, he was especially running. Even if you didn't do anything wrong and you looked at the coaches the wrong way, you were told to "run a suicide;" reminding me of *Remember the Titans* when anything went wrong and Denzel said, "You will run a mile."

With all this running we were doing, it just gave me a flashback of the previous year; we were only down by a couple of points at half-time, but I remember coming in at half-time and so many people exasperated and breathing extremely hard, including myself. Everyone's legs were burning. The previous day, we had practice at school and then went to the Illinois gym to shoot around that night.

That really gave our bodies aches and pains the next day. It definitely showed because when we came out at halftime, Illinois gave it to us. They blew us out and there was nothing that we could do about that; we had nothing left in the tank. We were talking about how we needed that game for the Big Ten championship because they beat us earlier in the year at our place in overtime, so we needed to steal one back from them.

Chapter 15

A Big Hart

For the Illinois game, Coach Painter changed up the starting line up and took Kramer and me out of the starting five. Illinois is another tough team to guard. Our teams had a lot of similarities, but they had a frontcourt that could shoot just as well as their guards. They knew how to take away our shot- blocking, and our rebounding. They gave us so many problems throughout the past games when we played them at home, away or even on neutral courts; it didn't matter the location, they always shot well against us. When we watched them on TV, we always wondered why they rarely shot poorly against us.

This was always an intense game because of the history between our coaches and the defensive similarities between our teams. Coach Weber use to coach at Purdue when Coach Painter was a player, so Coach Painter, due to his competitive nature, was intent on trying to out-shine him. Illinois had one of the best home courts in the Big Ten, as well as in the nation. The fans were right on top of us the moment we stepped onto the court for warm-up.

The game bounced up and down, but we got one of the biggest lifts in a single game performance that I had seen since Marcus Green kept us in the game against Michigan State his senior year. John Hart came out with a bang; this was his first real action and he took full advantage of his opportunity. John was hitting three-pointers, getting key rebounds, blocking shots, and doing it all. It was exactly what we needed to happen for us to make the game go in our favor. He got a career high of fourteen points. He was the player to watch in that game and earned his few minutes of fame when he was interviewed on ESPN with Erin Andrews.

When he entered the locker room after his interview, we jumped him in a form of gratitude to show that his performance was definitely needed and much appreciated.

Old Man Wisdom #16

I think that John is a prime example of what is meant by being prepared at all times when your number is called to go into the game; how you need to perform when your opportunity presents itself. That is exactly what he did when he went into the game. On the white board, Coach Painter wrote something very interesting for John's area of needed improvement. He wrote, "Have your shoes tied," and he explained that he needed to be ready for however and

whenever it's time for him to go into
the game to produce positive results.

Now that we were back at .500, we still had a long Big Ten season ahead of us to get where we desired to be, so we needed to handle each and every game like we were playing for a championship. After the Northwestern loss, I told the team that that was the last lost of the season; we didn't need any more lessons to get back on the right track. We simply needed results from each and every player.

Chapter 16

Unique Michigan

We played the unique Michigan team, and the reason I call them unique is because we never knew what Michigan team we were going to play; if they felt like showing up and playing to their full capability, then they could be tough because of their level of talent. Now, on the other hand, they could be easy to beat because sometimes they sabotaged themselves by not playing well together. They beat Duke earlier in the year. Then they lost to a team by twenty points, a team they could have beaten very easily. We would see which team was going to show up. We only played them once just like Northwestern, so the game was even more significant.

Before the game, when we were being taped, we heard that Manny Harris did not make the game. Manny usually scored about twenty points. This was about twenty points that would be missing from the score board. Just the absence of his scoring, rebounding skill and his court presence alone could have potentially hurt the Michigan team. We would have our hands full against them, knowing that DeShawn Sims would be even more aggressive than usual. JJ had that assignment starting the game, so his hands were full. Ironically, as we were waiting for the announcer to call the starting lineups, JJ whispered in my ear," Make sure that you lock up who you are guarding."

The game started and Sims stole the show, scoring the first eleven points for Michigan. I said to myself, "*Who* needed that advice that JJ just gave me?" Sims was giving JJ what Sims wanted; spin moves, three-pointers, pull-ups, pretty much anything he wanted to do. We did not get in his way. When we got into the locker room for half-time, all I could do was go in there with a smile on my face. JJ looked at me, smiled and said, "KG, don't say anything!" We laughed about it because he knew as well as anyone on the team what he needed to do. Sims definitely got the memo that Manny Harris, who was the leading scorer on the team, was not playing. Sims had a great first half.

JJ gained control of Sims' scoring and took control of the game, and we pushed the lead out to twenty seven points in the second half at one point. Down the stretch, to close out the game, we had turnovers and were taking bad shots, which cut the lead in half. We still won, but we knew we had to do better when it concerned closing out games.

E'twaun spoke to Manny afterward and asked why he did not attend the game. Manny said he was kicked out of practice for throwing an elbow in, but the elbow was not on purpose.

Chapter 17

Back Home Again at Purdue

This was the second of a three home game stretch. Due to the way that we started the Big Ten season, we needed this three game stretch to get in a good rhythm and get in the flow of things. We always get in a better rhythm when we play at home. We had a huge game against Wisconsin, a game that weighed so much because they already beat us earlier at their place. Wisconsin was always at the top of the Big Ten standings and they would be in the running for Big Ten regular season champs. We definitely needed to handle our business at home and not let them come in to our home court and steal one.

There were two key factors to this game: Taylor, their guard came off the bench to score twenty three points. Taylor now started because John Luers got injured in our game. Second, what we needed to contain was their one-on-one plays that they made when their swing offense broke down. They dominated us with one-on-one plays at their place. Taylor singlehandedly outscored our bench, so we had to keep him in check this game. Bohannon also had twenty points and even though Hughes was in foul trouble, he would always find a way to score.

I was enthusiastic about this game against Wisconsin; not only was it an important game, but my homeboy Lewis "Decatur" Jackson was returning from his foot injury to rejoin the team. You always want to have a player like Lewis whose sole purpose is to be a fierce competitor; a player who will do anything to win. What's amusing about it was that Trevon Hughes must have heard that Lewis was coming back because as we were walking out to get some shots up before our team warm-up, he asked him in a concerned voice if he was returning.

I fully understand why he asked that question; Lewis had ability to play defense full court. He was only 5'9 but he was strong and quick, and his center of gravity was so solid. I hated when he guarded me in practice, and felt sorry for anyone who had to deal with him for a 40-minutes game, especially when it is not just practice and the game. It felt good to know that we were already in their heads before the game started.

The thing that Lewis and I were discussing was his concern about coming back and getting injured again. If that happened, he would have given up a whole season after only playing that one game. But he made a mature decision, and I had to take my hat off to him because he sacrificed a great deal to play again, even if for a very short season. He could have redshirted instead and still enjoyed another year. This is the true definition of a selfless player. It takes guts to do what Lewis did. He knew that he would not be in the best of shape to truly perform for the team. I know from experience that it is not comfortable out on the court when returning after an injury. It feels like everyone is so much faster and what you are doing is not effective.

Lewis was brought into the game for me and the Paint Crew and the crowd went crazy and screamed, "LEW...!!!!" It gave *me* goose bumps and I'm not Lewis! I don't know how he held it together. I was just so happy to see him out there playing again with us. He got into a pick and roll situation and he went in for the layup because the opposing defense stayed with the big man, and he scored his first points of the season. The sold-out crowd went crazy and so did the players on the bench. I looked over to see his mother with the biggest smile on her face. It was a Kodak moment.

The game was an up-and-down event. It came down to what we preach about in practice, about one stop to win the game. We needed to have strong determination and make sure that we locked up on the final possession. We were ahead by one point, and they had the ball. This prompts a flashback to my sophomore year; we were in a similar situation at a home game, Rob made a good block at the buzzer to seal our fate, and the Paint Crew rushed the floor. Back to the present; Hughes had possession of the ball and put up a floater. From my viewpoint, it looked great, but it hit the backboard and then the front of the rim and bounces off. JJ grabbed the rebound and he is fouled immediately. Victory was sealed with that rebound. We needed that game more than they did. With Lewis back, it made us deeper in the back court and gave us even more speed for the fast break.

Going into the last game of the home stretch against Penn State, we heard about Coach Painter having contract issues. The rumor was that he was threatening to move on if he didn't get a contract extension. This was a potential distraction to the team. It is essential to keep distractions to a minimum when dealing with teams. All the great teams that usually win championships rarely have major distractions or anything that takes the focus off of the team. I wanted to ask a couple of the teammates if they heard anything about this ordeal. Truthfully, it was none of my concern, and I was apprehensive about spreading inaccurate information. Our focus needed to be on Penn State and nothing else, so I just kept it to myself and hoped that it did not circulate further than where it originated. I was going to let a **bad rumor** stay as a **bad rumor**.

Penn State has a high-quality guard in Talor Battle. Penn State was and always had been a good rebounding team, but they were 0-8 in conference play. The previous year at Penn State, we were plus eight on the offensive rebounding column before the first TV time out. This speaks volumes about our lack of effort on the glass in that game, how big they are on the interior and how much they wanted that game that night. We definitely could not let that happen on this night. We had to knock their confidence down early and not let them get into the game. They'd had some close games but lost them. We were victorious and held the rebounding in check. We refused to let Battle get off like he usually does against other teams.

Chapter 18

What's a Hoosier to do?

This was a game that the whole state of Indiana had been awaiting. Both our fans and their fans were anticipating this competing between two teams with a history of one of the biggest rivals in college basketball. The Hoosiers versus the Boilermakers; what a game this was going to be. It was being played at Assembly Hall, one of three buildings in which I had never enjoyed victory. The huge rival game at IU brought "at war" looks on our coaches' faces. As far as the fans were concerned, this was the single most important game of the year. We had chants that the Paint Crew ended with "IU Sucks." Indiana was just as intense with that too, as if they had so much pain in their hearts when they said, "Purdue". Also when a person came into the Mackey arena wearing an Indiana shirt, the crowd would point them out and scream, "IU sucks" and jokingly says "kick them out." I have seen a person take off his shirt because he was getting harassed by our loyal fans so badly.

The coaches had been sending text messages out from former players containing Coach Keady's motivational words from when he was coaching the Boilermakers. We even received text messages regarding what Coach Knight had said about the rivalry when he used to go head to head with Coach Keady. All of the texts had been personal and directed towards the rivalry between the two schools.

Assembly Hall was a unique gym; it had theater seating and gave teams the feeling of putting on a show like they were at the opera. What's amusing is that the IU team and our team were staying in the same hotel. For all four years I had been playing, we had never stayed in the same hotel as the other team when on the road in the conference. We were watching film and eating dinner, and we heard them watching a movie as if they needed lines of motivation. The thing that made it even more interesting was that it seemed like they had turned up the volume of the movie just to annoy us.

Jeremiah Rivers and I played on the same AAU team in Florida and he was their starting point guard, so it was going to make the game even more fun. One of the biggest reasons why I had been looking forward to this game was because one of the freshmen, Waterford, had been boasting so much in the summer workouts when we were at the same gym. He was dominating the guy on my team when we were playing 3-on-3 and he knew I played for Purdue. He said, "I am going to do Purdue the same way." I said, "Those are big words coming from a person who hasn't played in the Big Ten and trust me, you will not beat us, because your team is not ready for a team like ours. You might be able to do something in these workouts, but you are not ready for someone like Rob." When it was time for the game, I made sure to brief the whole team on what he'd said.

The IU fans also made sure that it was known that they hated Purdue; they had posters of different players' faces waving throughout the student section. It took a while to get accustomed to seeing them, but that was one of the first places that we played where they had the big face posters, even though we saw it all the time on ESPN. I came off the bench and when I got into the game, I scored a quick five points; during the next dead ball, I was taken out. I couldn't understand for the life of me why I was pulled out. I was just starting to get a rhythm.

"I got taken out;" these are the things I have to fight in my head, saying to myself "Why the hell did I just get taken out?" Maybe it is for the better of the team, but I couldn't fathom how because I came in the game and scored a quick five points in the first two minutes. I was in there playing great defense. I sat on the bench for a good portion of the first half. I was thinking, maybe he is teaching me a lesson of some sort from when we lost the three games in a row, but I just couldn't comprehend why. I tried to keep my mind focused on the game, which is difficult to do when you have conflicting thoughts like this going through your head.

In the first half, our rival had so many easy layups and dunks, and they kept scoring off the same play time after time. They had the lead at the end of the first half, and the coaches came into the locker room yelling, "Why are you not following the game plan?"

Old Man Wisdom #17

In my head, I'm thinking that they definitely are not referring to me because I was barely on the court, but when you are the captain and leader of the team, you cannot allow yourself to think in a selfish manner. You must put the team first, and that is so difficult at times. You have to push your teammates on and show the younger players how they can do better and where they need to improve for your team to be victorious.

I stayed focused on the game even though I did not play much the second half. Of course, as a competitor, you are never happy when your playing time is cut. Despite our opponents getting a lot of easy buckets in the second half, and the crowd roaring so loud that we could barely hear ourselves think, we still kept the composure that comes with experience and camaraderie. Even through the roaring of the crowd, we just remained settled and played our game down the stretch. The concentration on our faces was so great, it was beautiful; we were on a mission. Kramer and I had a goal: We wanted to play out this year winning in every gym where we had played in the Big Ten. The game came down to one of the final plays where we were trading baskets down the stretch. I'm in the game at the end, which means my coaches still had confidence in me to get the job done. Coach Painter told me to pick up the point guard but not to foul. I execute his instructions, and they went down the court. Their big man set a screen to get Jones open. He shot a three-pointer that would have sent the game into overtime. I was thinking as I was watching the shot, *we definitely do not want it to go to overtime*; we had not won a game in overtime as long as I could remember. But fortunately, it missed! We won the game; Kramer and I got another notch in our road trip win goal. Coach Painter told me after the game that that's why it's important that I don't give the point guard any space when coming up the court. The idea is for them not to get a clean look, and as a result, they will have to use more clock than what they want to use. So I made a mistake. I learned a valuable lesson, not to let anyone get open.

We usually got food right after the game, but whenever we played in Bloomington, we waited until we were about thirty to forty-five minutes up the road. My theory was there was so much rivalry between the two schools that the coaches never wanted to put their players in any harm. Go figure.

Chapter 19

Wishes Do Come True

Another arena where Kramer and I had not yet won is Breslin Center: Home of Michigan State basketball, but I planned to make that happen. I planned on achieving that goal this time around so we could stay in the hunt for a top spot in the Big Ten. Every game in the conference was crucial because there were certain games that would have so much implication at the end of the Big Ten season. Some games determined if your team would walk away with a Regular season championship, and this was one of those games. The last time we were at Michigan State, it was their senior night and they really worked us. They did not even give us a chance to get our heads up. They finished a team like they were supposed to finish at home, on senior night, securing them a Big Ten regular season championship.

This would be the first time that we were playing them, first on the road as they usually came to our place first, and then we would finish at their place on the last game of the Big Ten season. When Michigan State is at home, they have one of the biggest advantages, because their student section was 360 degrees around the floor. They were out there about two hours before the game even started. So when we walked out on the floor to get some extra jump shots up, before we even started our routine of warm-ups as a team, they were there to heckle us. Of course, like any road game, they always went after Chris Kramer, saying that he was a faker or an actor. I have no clue but it never failed that they went after Kramer.

Kalin Lucas was not 100%; he twisted his ankle against Wisconsin, a game before ours, and decided to sit out the game against Illinois. That gave them a loss and we were definitely happy about it, because that put us closer than them in the standings for first place in the Big Ten. So if we could hand them another loss on their home court, we would be on our way to being in a good position at the end of the Big Ten season.

Lucas was in the game, but you could tell that he didn't have the explosiveness that he usually had; he was moving with a little limp. Chris Allen had a big first half on us, hitting shot after shot. I came in off the bench. I was so amped up that when I got in the game, JaJuan set me a screen; I go off the screen and I'm open for a three-point shot because they were going under the screens and *smack,* nothing but backboard. Knowing that my minutes have been limited lately I was expecting to come out; as soon as I look backed at the scorer's table to see what was going on, that is exactly what was happening, I was going straight to the bench.

Earlier in the year, that was something that was not happening. I had much more cushion with my playing time. It was something that I couldn't let be a distraction to my game. We had a good lead and they made their run down the stretch. Basketball is a game of runs, and we were able to withstand their run down the stretch. I couldn't be any happier, considering it was the first time ever winning in that building. Next up was one more building in which Kramer and I had not experienced a win: Columbus.

We got into the locker room after the game, and this was one of the few times when we would see our coach's dance; they only do so after a huge road victory, never at home. We would all get into a circle around Coach Lusk, and he did this one leg hop; it is the funniest thing. The plane ride back was full of nothing but laughter, which was how it should have been after a good win. Me, personally I was just glad to be on the plane headed back to West Lafayette.

Each year, it has never failed that when we go to East Lansing, there is a snowstorm. Last year was the worst. I could've sworn that we were going to crash; we had to make two landing attempts. We actually landed on the third time, and that attempt was so shaky, it had everyone just praying that we would land safe. So many people who were planning on attending the game were not able to make it and they lived in Michigan. I had given a ticket to Nate Minnoy, whom I played with my freshman year before transferring; he was not able to make it because of the terrible weather, I'm just thankful that we made it back safe.

Chapter 20

Mission Accomplished

Iowa came to town, and this game was nothing more and nothing less than a focused game. We needed to handle our business by not letting them get their heads up. We couldn't let them think that we were going to give them a chance to win.

Time out against Iowa; notice it is near Valentine's Day....
the Love for JJ in the crowd ....
my Haiti Fund raising shirt

Iowa was a team, which has had to overcome big distractions with one of their best players by the name of Anthony Tucker. We heard that Tucker was returning back to the team after being indefinitely suspended for a drinking incident. During the shoot around, Coach Lusk walked in and said, "KG, guess what?" I say, "What's up?" Coach said, "Tucker decided to transfer." I was in disbelief. After the school and the team had showed so much interest in keeping him around and giving him a second chance, it was surprising to hear. We also heard that there were plenty of players on the Iowa team who might be very unhappy.

Old Man Wisdom #18

At the end of the day, we cannot be worried about them; we only can control what we do and be focused on the game and that is it.

To complete the whole mission of winning in every venue in the Big Ten, the last stop was Ohio State. We had played a couple overtime games there but had never escaped with a victory. Ohio State has an NBA kind of arena; it is so big, at times it won't even get loud. They beat us at home and we definitely needed to get that win back, especially because we had been at home and were winning the majority of the games, but we just fell apart the last three minutes of the game.

You could tell that Ohio State was a football school. The team was ranked #4 at the time and the arena was still not packed out. I thought that I had caught the flu, because I had been having a fever and had been really sluggish all

week. My athletic trainer had been giving me medication, trying to help me get better for the game. The previous year, we had the same exact problem, but there were about four of us who were sick. At least this year, it was just me.

Evan Turner had gone a little crazy on us the last time we played Ohio State at home, and it was only his second game back from his time off for his back injury. Evan finished with 32 points against us and Rob finished with 35 points, (29 of those points were in the first half). We still lost, so we definitely needed to get something back.

Despite being sick, I had been doing everything in my power to get energy and assist my team to a victory. I had eleven points in the first half to give us a boost. During that first half, we jumped out on them and sustained a lead on them. They made a big push in the second half to take the lead. We were talking as a group. *"Why doesn't Jeremy Simmons or P.J Hill play anymore?"* At one point in time, they were a key piece of the puzzle and went from playing all the time to not even getting in the game. Four of their players played forty minutes. Rob said he saw in the highlights on ESPN that when one of the Ohio State players was shooting, he saw Simmons and Hill playing on the bench, inattentive to what was going on in the game. We remembered what they did the year before towards the end of the game. When the game was already decided, they threw it off the backboard to rub it in our faces even more. Turner had a good game against us, but no one else had a good game like they usually did. Evan did not shoot the ball well; he had 28 points off of 21 shots.

We pulled the game out and Kramer and I would finish our careers by doing something that not too many seniors who played all four years in the Big Ten can say that they have accomplished; to win in every venue in the Big Ten. During the game, I remembered scoring a layup on Lauderdale, and I fell as I was hitting the layup. Rob and I were talking about that on the plane on the way back to school. I remember when it happened because they took the ball out fast and tried to get a fast break; it took so much energy and I did not want to get up because I was already sick. I definitely did not want to run back on defense and guard Evan Turner. Rob said he could see on my face that I wanted to pass out; he said he was caught between going back to his man and staying with Turner. He said "KG, you took forever to get back in front of him." He was laughing so hard when he retold me the story. I just wanted the game to be over.

But at the end of the game, we were up by only three. Buford went for a layup and I tried to cut him off. I didn't want to foul him and give him a chance to make a three-point play. Kramer came out of nowhere and blocked him. The ball got hit to Diebler and we scrambled. We tried to get them to take a tough shot and not have an easy look just to hit a three-point shot. If we went into overtime; as I had said, we do not perform well when we go to overtime, especially in this building. So, it came to Diebler having the ball in his hands for a last-second shot; He was the best three-point shooter on the Ohio State team, and I saw that no one was in front of him to contest the shot. I rushed to jump up to try to block the ball; took everything in me to do so. As I jumped, I caught a cramp in my calf muscle. I saw the ball go up, almost like in slow motion, like what you would watch on TV when you see a last second shot

that was on the line, but thank God he missed. I was so relieved that we did not have to play an extra five minutes, because I do not think I would have made it.

Chapter 21

Feeling some New Rivalries

This game was against Illinois, but it was in Mackey Arena, a place where we rarely got defeated. We had similar styles of play and it was not an easy team to play against. When we win against Illinois, our scouting report scheme is good and we play to our capability. Demetri McCamey had one hell of a game against us at their place with 28 points. The first of the game, we made McCamey a passer and made sure that he did not get any easy looks. I think that we went above and beyond and did a poor job of taking other things away, because he had eleven assists in the first half.

The thing that usually gives us a big boost is our crowd, but we had low energy and it was against Illinois! We definitely should not have had low energy because the crowd was always top-notch when playing Illinois. Their fans travel to games and we were still in the hunt for trying to get a Big Ten regular season championship and we did not want to get a rude awakening by losing, especially not on our home court. In the second half, we got it together. I actually scored 13 points.

JaJuan had a rare struggle in this game; he was usually on top of his game when we played Illinois, but he went 1 for 10 from the field. E'twaun was Mr. Clutch, so smooth and calm at all times and never let too many things play him out of his game. Down the stretch, he hit tough shots to keep us in a good position to win. We cranked it up on defense in the second half and Rob finished the game with a double-double. Kelsey seemed to not be in the game quite as much, as if he was distracted by something. Lewis was still finding his way on offense; searching to catch a rhythm. But an area where Lewis would never struggle or need to improvement is his rhythmic ball defending. You can tell how he hassles the opponent; how much frustration he puts on the opponents' point guards. We pulled a big one out at home and after the game, Coach Weber whispered in my ear, "When you play like you're capable of playing, you make a difference." That comment sat ingrained in my consciousness that night as I contemplated what he told me.

Even though everyone did not play well and we had low energy to start the game, we still found a way to win with our defense; we relied on each other to pull their weight and do what was asked of us; these are the qualities of a championship team.

It was February 22nd and I was watching games as a fan. Today was a good day because Ohio State beat Michigan State, at State's home court, which rarely happened. It was unheard of for Michigan State to lose at home, but Ohio State prevailed over them this day, which aided our cause even more. With the victory that Ohio State pulled, it allowed us to reach number one in the Big Ten standings, alone, at the moment. To seal the game, Jon Diebler hit a three-point shot. As soon as he did, I jumped up in my apartment as if I was an alumnus of the Buckeyes. As a team, we watched games throughout the nation and checked out rankings on a regular basis. At least I did. With Villanova losing this day, it also helped us to move up in the polls. We kept pushing but we had much more to do. Things were looking bright for us to get a number one seed if we kept on the same focus level.

Some of the players from Minnesota made remarks in the papers and on their local news about what was going to happen and what they were going to display on the court when we played them. Damian Johnson said that "we" were overrated and were not worthy of all the hype that we got in the media around that time. They were going to show the nation that they were one of the nation's best. The funny thing was that those quotes were actually in October or November.

The game just added more fuel to the fire, because we thought that we didn't get enough recognition and knew that our focus needed to be on the prize; Minnesota was going to come out and play hard, rebound and try to embarrass us. We were in the "barn;" it would be loud and we would barely be able to hear ourselves think. The road games were just as important as the home games. The team in the Big Ten that wins the most road games, 9 times out of 10, would win the conference title.

My teammates were keeping better track than I was on how much closer I was to scoring 1,000 points. According, to them, I only needed 35 more; they were relaying this to me as we were headed to our hotel. While checking into our rooms, Lewis approached me and was grinning nervously. As we were getting off the bus and getting our bags to go into the hotel, a big gust of wind came and almost knocked a couple people over. Coach

Keady's baseball cap flew off his head and Coach Paint had to catch himself as the wind knocked him into the bags on the curb. The wind in Minnesota did not play fair.

Everyone shot with precision in the first half, but Rob was on fire. It was not like his back-to-back three pointers and pull-up jump shots, as in the game against Ohio State, but he was shooting the ball skillfully. Midway through the first half, Rob drove to the right towards me. He jumped and stopped to take a shot, but his legs gave out; he laid there in pain and agony. From my vantage point, it appeared that his knee just buckled. It had happened to me a few times.

I went to take a long look at him; it was obvious that he was in immense pain. But we had to block that out because there was still a game to win. He went into the locker room with the athletic trainer. I had this feeling that maybe it could be a little serious. I just got this feeling based on the way the trainer looked like there was something that he was not telling Rob. We brushed it off; it *was* Rob. It was probably just a hyper-extension, and we figured he would be back a couple of weeks later.

We went back out for the second half of the game; we would take care of business and get out of there with a victory, but then we went ten minutes without scoring a single field goal! Our opponents went on a 19-0 run to get back in the game. John Hart came in and gave us a spark, which he usually did when he was in the game. We fought back to the last minute to get out of there successfully. It came down to seven seconds left on the clock. E'twaun drove and kicked it to Lewis; Lewis drove the baseline on the left side. As he drove, he jumped to make a pass to me. I swept left because the defender chased me off the three-point line; I took a one dribble pull-up and it went in, bottom of the net. We took the lead with that shot and the opposing team called a time-out. They got a chance to win, but failed at the buzzer. I will always remember that shot. I knew that was one of the top three clutch shots I had ever taken and executed throughout my career.

Chapter 22

Rob: Never Dreamed *this* Might Happen...

The next day, in the morning I got a call from one of my friends from Florida, congratulating me on the shot, and he said, "You know your boy Hummel tore his ACL." I said, "How do you figure that?" "Because I tore my ACL and you can see on ESPN that the knee gave away and turned inward, the same way I did mine." I said, "We will see." I was praying that what he was predicting was not the case. I got up and turned on the TV. The first thing that I saw on ESPN was that Rob's knee did give away and turn inward like Chris, my friend from Florida, said it did.

Coach Painter called a team meeting and told us that Rob had torn his ACL and that he was out for the remainder of the season. It was as if someone had told us that we were held hostage, because there was total silence. He said what was done was done and we were still in the hunt for a championship. He warned us not to get crazy and try to play outside of our means, but everyone, as a whole, needed to come together and just do a little bit more to fill the gap. He advised us not to do things that we hadn't already been doing all season. If everyone brought more intensity to the table and played even harder, we would be fine.

After hearing the news, you could tell that some of the players were distracted and their morale was down. It was our off day, so after the meeting we were free to leave. The thing that bothered some of us was that some teammates were gathered in the team lounge, huddled together talking and looking extremely defeated and sad, as if someone had died. One of our key guys had a season-ending injury, and it was as if some of the other players were surrendering to the pressure. We were not a one-man team. It was unfortunate that an injury of that degree had to happen, but that was the risk in sports. We had an important upcoming match at home against Michigan State. They would know the news before game time; they were going to come in and try to snatch the game from us as we did at their place; this was not the time to doubt each other or wallow in self-pity. Rob certainly would not have wanted that.

The next day during practice, we began to discuss the game against Minnesota. We made light of a crucial time in the game when Patrick Bade drove and turned back to make a pass but threw it to the referee; he couldn't help but laugh at that, too. It was a much needed laugh for some of the players on the team, because some of them had not cracked smiles since they heard the news about Rob. But in that Minnesota game, Patrick showed what he was capable of doing and that we needed him to continue to keep doing it; being solid and battling the opponents' front court.

At the start of practice, we did our usual routine: film, walk through, and practice plays that we were going to do on offense and defense for our next game. The game was against Michigan State, and I would be playing the "four" man position on offense when we ran our plays. It would be an interesting game, because even though Rob got hurt in the Minnesota game, this would be the first full game we would play without him. We were reveling in the victory we had won against Michigan State and how we would be number one in the Big Ten, standing alone.

The game was a poor performance from both teams. Michigan State had 23 turnovers but still managed to out rebound us by 26. With Rob being out, this was the one game, out of many, where we needed to rebound as a whole, not relying on one person as we so often did. And now that that one person could no longer play for the rest of

the season, we had to do better. Otherwise, our season was going to be cut very short in the post season.

That night, we could have pointed at a lot of different areas that lost us the game. For starters, the most obvious was poor rebounding. In addition, we were not playing defense to our full capability, and lastly, we were playing *through* our offense. After the game, Coach noted that if we would have lost in the rebound column by 15, and not 26, we could have won the game. It was my responsibility to step up, and I definitely did not do that. I have to say I folded like a lazy boy, and Rob told me after the game that I had needed to be more aggressive and not pick my spot, which I usually did in the game.

One reason why we did not win was because we needed another scorer, and I did not step up. Also, a lot of the shots that we would usually make did not go in. There were plenty of our shots that went in bounced right back out; that is the main reason why we should not have played *through* our offense that night. We definitely made our defense the staple of the game. The majority of the time, shots were not going to fall, but we needed to find other ways to leave the game with a victory. We had been doing a good job of that throughout the year, but somehow this time, we dropped the ball, no pun intended.

As the game got down the stretch, E'twaun had a good look at a three-pointer, but like many of the shots of the night, it touched every part of the rim and popped back out. What *put* a lid on the game was when Michigan State would go down the floor, get a shot up, miss, and then Draymond Green would muscle his way for a key offensive rebound and would put it back in for a score.

After the game, I got home and I couldn't really sleep, which was typical for me after we lost games. My Mom, who was visiting with my Pops, came out and had a heart-to-heart talk with me. I really did not feel like listening to the lecture, but I stayed there and took her words to heart. She told me that I did not step up this game and the team desperately needed me. I was simply out there. "You did not want to take the game over like you are capable of doing," she said, "I know you have been in a slump, but you needed to find ways of scoring and making your team better. If your team is relying on you to do better, then you needed to step up to the plate, because this is your time." I think her words really hit home, just because your parents always want the best for you. And for my mom to come out and tell me this, it was a wakeup call to the reality that my team did need me. There needed to be no excuses; just me getting the job done. It was a long overdue chat. I definitely was not going to let her words go without action.

Chapter 23

Senior Night

The final game of year would be played in Mackey Arena. Senior night had arrived and I was to play the best team to end a career against: Indiana University. My family was still in town, so I definitely wanted to "show off" for my last game in Mackey. It was going to be a good night; the last time playing in front of the great fans of Mackey Arena and running out of the tunnel while the band plays; the last time, after a victory, that I would get to see the smiles on the students' faces after hard work on the court; giving them high fives after the game; the last time, after the game, you get to see all the players' families and the kids who want autographs; the last time I would walk in for my pregame ritual at home and hear "have a good one, KG" from my two friends who worked on the game usher committee.

As we ran out of the tunnel as a team, I could see on the board where the Paint Crew usually posted their hustle points that it read, "KG, 18K." (18 points to 1,000 career points.) It had been a long but short journey. Kramer and I had been a part of something really special there; helping get Purdue back to where it belonged; starting from a season before ours when they only won nine games. Each year that we had been there, we improved our win total and participated in the tournament each year, and we would do the same this year. We were excited to play IU on the last game of our careers at home.

We had a team bet that if I got a fast break, I would get a backwards dunk. So the first play of the game, IU won the tip and they get set up to run their offense. The point guard made a pass. I got a steal. I looked back to see if he was trailing me to try to block it. As I went to dunk it backwards, I got so excited that I lost the ball out of bounds. Ha! All I could do was laugh it off, because I knew I missed the opportunity to do it all by myself with fresh legs. I looked over to Rob, who was laughing like he was watching *America's Funniest Home Videos*. So after some "**not** top-ten playing," we jumped on them.

We were getting pretty much anything that we wanted on offense. I think I was so focused on getting to 1,000 points that it caused a distraction by making me so anxious. Kramer finished with a great game. In the hotel before the game, we had a discussion that Kramer would probably be the one who would get emotional during senior night and our teammates thought I would be the last person who would show any emotion. We were all wrong. I was the one who got emotional; as Ryne substituted in for me, and I raised my hands to the 14,000 plus fans embracing me, I walked off the court for the last time and the goose bumps crept all over my body. It was one of the most special and defining moments of my life. I will always have that joy in my heart.

I think I can speak for the seniors on the team by saying that we all appreciated the ceremony that was held after the game for us. Most of the fans stayed there to hear each of us speak and have our families presented to our fans. It was like what you see on TV when proud families stand next to the players with smiles on their faces. It gave me such pride to have my family next to me walking on the floor, watching my highlights being played and hearing my name being called for the last time, with all of my teammates on the side watching; that is what it is all about, being a part of something special and knowing you helped rebuild and build a new foundation for a program to get back where it belongs. Hopefully, we inspired younger players to join the Purdue family and carry on the greatness.

Sir Edmund Hillary, a Great Mountain Climber, Wisdom #1

If the going is tough and the pressure is on, if reserves of strength have been drained and the summit is still not in sight, then the quality to see in a person is neither great strength nor quickness of hand, but rather a resolute mind firmly set on its purpose that refuses to let its body slacken or rest....For you, my teammates, past, present and future, do not rest until you reach your goal....

Chapter 24

A lot at Stake.

It was the last game of the Big Ten season; a lot was at stake. We were at Penn State. They had been less than stellar all season, which meant that they would not play in the post season, so I would suspect they would aim to end their season with little joy at our expense. In my personal opinion, they were talented but did not consistently click together as a team. A win over them would give us a share of the regular Big Ten title. Usually, when I woke up before a game, all I could do was smile. When I did so, for no reason, it usually meant we were guaranteed to then win. I had the same feeling last year in the tournament when we played Washington.

I was in the hotel making my way to breakfast and I couldn't help smiling from ear to the ear. I got there and took a seat; Lewis and Mark were doing the same thing. I asked, "Why are you all so happy?" and they said, "Man, we are about to get another ring." We all talked about how none of the coaches and most of the players could not really get any sleep, because one of the goals we set at the beginning of the year was only forty minutes away, but it felt like it was eternity before the game started; everyone was on cloud nine.

We were nervous with the excitement of another Big Ten title in our reach *and* the Paint Crew having traveled to come show support. Looking around the arena, it appeared like we had more fans than they did. Talor Battle came by and talked to a group of us during warm-ups. We could not second guess why he was doing so. You would think that he should have been with his own team either talking or warming up.

Over the years, we sometimes let complacency set in and we gave up critical games. We had a similar situation last year but this year would be different; we had more of a "do or die" moment set before us. Either we were going to win or we were going to squander a lot of hard work that we had amassed; coming back from being in the hole in the first five Big Ten games with a 2-3 record; all that could be in the past with us just winning the last game on the road.

We came out playing well, and I came out on fire; I told my parents before the game started that there would be no more waiting, and this was the game that would take me to the 1,000 points and more. We built a big lead, but amazingly, in the last five minutes, we let it slip away. Talor Battle played limited minutes because of cramping of some sort, but they still managed to come back. It was down to one last shot on their part and one last stop on ours; all the guts and glory; what a way to end the season. Chris Baab came off a screen and took a shot, and I blocked it; I couldn't believe they called a foul. Baab tried to milk it with a little acting; the acting was an afterthought and they *still* called a foul. I guess the referees wanted to increase the excitement of the game. He hit all his free throws and tied the game, but they never took the lead and we won the game by four points. I wouldn't have been able to forgive myself if that foul would have cost us the game, even though I *did not* foul him.

We celebrated in the locker room, took pictures with the trophy like we just got married to it. You could say we were satisfied with our level of hard work and dedication over the course of the year. But we still could not be satisfied because our main goal was not only just to be Big Ten regular season champs, but to make it to a Final Four.

We were posing for the camera, holding fingers up to show we were going to get fitted for another ring, and thinking about how another banner would be hung at the start of the next season. We then went out to the court again where the fans that traveled from Lafayette along with the Boiler fans that live near Penn State stayed to see us with the trophy. We posed for plenty of pictures with them and thanked them for showing their support. We told them that the Big Ten championship was for them, too.

As you can imagine, the plane ride home is so much better when you win, especially with the championship. I was just so relieved that the foul did not have a horrendous effect on the game. As we were exiting the airport, there were more than five hundred fans waiting to see us. It is the best feeling to return home to a cheering crowd after winning a championship and holding the trophy up in the air. We walked out and boarded on the Boilermaker Special as Coach Paint and the seniors made speeches. The pride that the fans give us, when they do meaningful things like that, goes a long way.

We heard a lot of doubters, even from our own local reporters, that it would be such a long shot for us to come back and win the Big Ten title after such a lousy start. But we stuck together and we took on the motto "family first." During the celebration at the airport, I saw Kyle Coleman. He did not go on the road trip because he was not put on the travel team. He told me that Stevie Loveless quit, which was just his luck, because he missed out on a ring and he waited right up to the end of the season. With all the work that he had put in for so long, it seemed a shame. But everyone makes their decisions for themselves. This can be the best time of the whole year, the reason why you play; tournament time, "baby." We were the two seed in the Big Ten Tournament and we would anxiously wait to see who we would play, Indiana or Northwestern.

Chapter 25

Big Ten. Big Embarrassment.

We were scheduled to play Northwestern. Around this time, when teams don't have a chance to make it to the tournament, they usually go on "vacation" early. Northwestern just conquered IU. I was glad that we were playing Northwestern because this was the only team in the Big Ten that we had not defeated that year. We would have the opportunity to get a little back for them beating us in the early part the year, with their fans honoring us by storming the floor. We really hadn't had to worry about them playing their zone against us. They hadn't done much of that throughout the year against us; they mostly played man-to-man, but their zone could be dangerous when they played it, because it was more like an "open gym" type zone, considering they would bait you into making bad plays. It was a fairly aggressive zone that extended to half court and got you as soon as you passed over half court, and sometimes a little bit before.

This was the first game for us in the Big Ten tournament, and I was limited to only fifteen minutes because I was dealing with cramping. I couldn't understand that because I drank plenty of fluids before the game. It didn't matter what I would do, I would develop cramps. They were everywhere; my stomach, hamstring, and I even caught one in my inner thigh which has never happened to me before. Northwestern was a very talented and unorthodox team. Shurna, who has an unorthodox game and did not look like he has played a game of basketball in his life, could definitely play because he had a good one-dribble pull up and was crafty around the basket. Toward the end of the game, while we were trying to close in on them, I was still cramping heavily, trying to go shoot free throws. I was barely able to walk. I actually heard the crowd laugh at me as I attempted to shoot. It was not funny at the time but I did laugh about it after the game. I wanted to be out there so badly to help my team, but I wasn't able to do so. Every time I told coach that I was ready to go in, I would go in and 30 seconds later, I was checking myself out because I was not able to move. The last time I went to the free throw line, before coach said I was not going in anymore, I heard a joke about how I was walking like Sanford, from the show **Sanford and Son**. Who wouldn't laugh at that? You have to keep a sense of humor; I was the

"Old Man" of the bunch. We won, even though the game got away from us toward the end, but we were able to manage their scrapping to win the game.

Next, we faced Minnesota again. They were fighting to get into the NCAA Tournament and we were looking for a back-to-back Big Ten-Tournament Championship. All the teams in the Big Ten had a reputation, maybe not a good one, but they were known to talk the most trash. The game started and we came out with very low energy, which was rare when it came to the tournament, but, they had our number that day! All I could say was, "wow." They were extremely big on the front line; they started with two seven-footers. Nothing was going to stop them this day. Anything that they wanted on offense, they got with very little effort, and we struggled to get the little bit we did. Minnesota beat us *so* bad and *so* fast we didn't even have a chance. They beat the brakes off us. The only thing that we felt was the embarrassment from the whooping Minnesota put on us. Coach pulled the starters, except JaJuan, out in the first five minutes of the second half. In my mind, all that I could think was, "Why is JaJuan out there; we do not need him to get hurt on a game that is already out of hands." Our team got pummeled that day. I remember us being stuck on four points and their score just kept going up and up and up. It was *the* worst loss *in* the worst fashion our team had since I had been at Purdue; one game that I hoped they just threw the film out and not make anybody watch, because, for damn sure, I didn't want to hear the feedback on this one.

We got beat by twenty-seven points. The only thing that you could take out of this game as a positive was that our reserves got plenty of playing time; real game time experience which they could carry to the NCAA tourney. One of the reserves who got a good rhythm going during the game was D.J. Byrd and the shots that he hit; he could use that confidence during tournament play. The worst thing about the game, besides suffering an embarrassing loss, was that Lewis had the two screws in his foot stepped on by Ralph Sampson III. He just stayed there rolling around on the ground; Lewis is a tough man and I have never seen him show so much pain on his face, not even when he first incurred the injury (Chris Kramer landed on his foot). This was the first time I had ever seen Lewis shed any tears over an injury. I just hoped that everything would be okay with him and that he would be able to play in the tournament. With that embarrassment over, we got a day off, I guess to reflect on the game. Then we could look forward to selection Sunday.

We always did selection Sunday at Coach Painter's house. He would order BBQ, all of the coaches and their families would come over; we relaxed and ate and watched where we were headed for the tournament. It was always exciting to see where you were going to be playing and who you would face; this was what the season and the hard work was all about. Not everyone in college basketball gets to experience this, so we felt privileged to be in the position to do so. I have been able to do that for four straight years. We were in the last bracket to be called; we were joking, "what happens if they forgot to put us in the bracket; how much hell would be raised if something like that took place?" We were the fourth seed in the South Bracket. The first team that we would face was Siena; the analysts from CBS already pegged us losing in the first round. We got a slap in the face before the tournament even started. They couldn't even wait a couple games; they wanted to fuel our fire before we even played the game. We thanked them for the extra motivation.

We headed out to Spokane, and started the tourney knowing that we had to win or go home. I was thinking, any loss after this point, and my career is over and all I could say then is, "I wish." Siena was a very talented team; they had the number one assist leader in the nation as well as very solid role and star players. They liked to get out in transition and they could rebound the ball well, which everyone knows was a major weakness in our game. We had to get used to playing on the west coast time, so Coach always scheduled practices around the time that we played, which was 11:30 west coast time, 2:30 Lafayette time, on Friday. It was a good thing to be playing so early because we could get the win and relax for the rest of the day.

As we played, I start to notice that fast breaking for them was really their only offense; they didn't have a lot of set plays. But they used the pick and roll and they were good at it. If you did not keep their point guard out of the paint, then it was going to be a long day for you. They had a big time scorer in Ubilies and a good, physically skilled number four man, a center who was crafty around the basket and averaged double digits in rebounding. He would be a good challenge for us right off the bat. They were hanging with us during the first half; we didn't have a good first half and at halftime, they were leading us by three points. At halftime, a lot of people on the team were complaining that it was hard for them to breathe; I didn't know if it was because we hadn't played in a week or because we were playing in a western state at a higher altitude. We decided that during the first five minutes of the second half, we had to dominate and put them on their heels. I, personally, wanted to make sure that we did not lose in the first round, and I was going to do everything in my power to make sure that we did not go home that day.

The second half was a different story; I don't know what got into me, but I came out and scored the first eleven of a thirteen-zero run. On defense, we added pressure with so many different people guarding their point guard full court. His coach liked to play him the whole game, and we used that to our advantage; we just wore him out. You could see the fatigue on his face; how much he was gasping for air. We turned up that Boilermaker defense and I am sure they had never seen that before. We hit them hard and they were unable to counter it. They made a little push at the end and tried to give us a scare, but it was not enough.

So we advanced to the next round where we would face Texas A&M. In the press, we kept hearing that President Obama felt *sorry* for us. In our minds, we were thinking, please don't, because we are not feeling sorry for ourselves and we had come to win. We wanted to prove him wrong; we now had something to prove to the entire nation.

During the tournament, usually all the other teams in your conference who are the regular season enemies, become fans of each other because they are in the same conference as you; you want to see your conference do well and go as far as it can. We were at the same site with Michigan State to play so we were rooting each other on; they were at our game and watched us play against Siena, and we watched their game in the locker room when they played before us. We saw them when we went out to practice at the arena, and we saw them before we went out to the floor. We wished them good luck and they did the same; it made me wonder if we had seen Minnesota, would it have been the same situation? It would have been interesting to see how each team would have reacted; wounds go deep sometimes, deeper than conference loyalty.

Chapter 26

The Big and Last Dance

Texas A&M was a good rebounding team, of course, and was similar to Michigan State. Anytime we faced a team who was good at rebounding, especially offensive rebounding, and had a big front line, it was always going to be a challenge for us. Their leading scorer was Sloan; he was one of the leading scorers in the Big Twelve; a big man who could score with his back to the basket. The game got underway and we went back and forth in the beginning, but we went in at halftime and were down by eleven points. In the locker room, we were relaxing and talking amongst ourselves about what we had to do better in the second half. There was a different vibe in the locker room for some reason this time, we were much calmer. I looked around and people were laughing and more anxious to go back out there and handle business. The coaches even seemed more relaxed at this point, still knowing that we were down by eleven. I told Coach Ray that he over-hyped Sloan; the person who I had been guarding the majority of the first half and would continue to do so the second half. He said, "KG, show me, show me that I am wrong; lock his ass up." I told him to watch and see.

During the second half, when the starters had not really been getting the job done, especially on defense, the reserves came in and turned the game all the way around and gave us the momentum. They were scoring, rebounding, and getting stops on defense; really giving us a lift. Now all that needed to happen was for the starters to return to the court and take us home. As a senior, I could not be more proud of them for giving us the lift that we needed. We came in and didn't skip a beat from where the reserves left off. It was heading down to the wire. We got a stop and we were in control. We had the ball with seconds to go and with a basket, we would win the game. E'twaun had the ball to set up for a one-on-one move; he was dribbling; he had the defender at one point go past him, but he lost the ball; they jumped on it and time ran out. They double-teamed him and he was unaware there were people open, but he wasn't able to see us because he was trying to recover the ball.

We went to overtime, and anyone who had ever followed us throughout the years knew that we were not that good and had little luck in overtime. I whispered to Kramer and told him that our season did not end here, and he agreed. Overtime is the same as regulation; we went back and forth and it came down to the end. We drew up a play and, of course, they took it away and Kramer took it himself and made the game-winning layup. I watched the play on ESPN. I had not seen it when it happened. It all happened so fast because when I passed Kramer the ball, he was supposed to pass to E'twaun, but he took off to the basket; my back was turned. I was the last person in the arena to know what was going on, but I was happy to know that the ball went in and we took the lead. They went in transition; all I was saying in my head was, "no March Madness on us, please?" They took it full court. There was a pass to the other guard; we played it pretty well, and they still got a good look for a fade away three. I was under the basket watching him shoot the ball, and everything at this point is slow motion. He launched it. I was saying, "Lord, oh Lord, he can't hit this." It was on line with the rim; it sailed toward the basket; my head was saying that it can't go in; they stormed the court as it ended up being short and we jumped for joy; we would go on to play another day.

I know they were heartbroken, I had to tip my hat off to them because they played well and hard. Both teams played their hearts out and I know for a fact that the fans, there and at home, enjoyed the game, because as a player, I enjoyed and appreciated the effort made by both teams put in and you could see that neither team wanted to go home. The guard who attempted the desperation shot was still lying on the floor after we had already shaken hands; it took one of the assistant coaches to pick him up because he was so emotional. I know I would have been in the same position if I were him and had played the way he played with his team.

We got back to the locker room and celebrated a second straight Sweet Sixteen bid. All of our families and friends were counting on us to win the game so that they wouldn't lose their money, because they had already ordered their tickets to go to Houston to watch us play. A lot of the teams' families were not able to make it to the Spokane site because there were no hotel rooms available and the airport was not close to where we had played.

We headed out to Houston to have a rematch with the Duke Blue Devils; we played them a year before where they embarrassed us on our home court. They were more physical and played harder than us. This time would be guaranteed to be a different scenario. They were a good all-around team; they had great size and good guards, but we were confident that if we played like we were capable of playing, we could get the job done. Of course we were undersized compared to other teams, so our guards had to make a special effort on the glass to help out JaJuan. We had gone through the scouting report numerous times, so we pretty much knew what play the coach would call next when they were going through things on tape and during walk through. We were playing at the Houston Texans' Reliant stadium; we played in a similar venue last year, where the Arizona Cardinals played. We did not shoot well in that type of venue. The venue has no close background like a regular arena does and like we were used to playing; it's like shooting at a rim in space. There is no good goalpost definition, and it gave a bad shooting feeling. When we walked in this "gym" this time, it was different; it wasn't so cavernous. It had a dark background, so it seemed like it was going to be a lot better this time around. The floor was elevated like a stage for the main event.

Going out there to take shots during the media shoot-around for an hour felt good; the electricity coursing through my body with the excitement and anxiousness to get on the court was an indescribable feeling.

Game time was here and as we walked into our locker room, we saw the score of Baylor and St. Mary's. The winner of that game would play the winner of our game. We looked at the score and we thought it was a mistake; it was a complete blow-out; Baylor was putting their foot on St. Mary's throats. We thought it was going to be a better game than that. Their game was over and as we went out to the court to warm up, one of the Reliant employees said to us, "Man, Duke is going to kill y'all, y'all have no chance!" Here we go again...us against the world, the underdog role. We knew we just had to go out there and shock the world. The place was packed; over 45,500 in attendance. I saw Avery Johnson and Chris Brown, to name a few in the crowd. It was a much-hyped game; some of my family was in attendance, and I was feeling good. The game started and we began with a strong campaign. We were down by 1 at halftime because Nolan Smith hit a jumper to give our opponents the lead.

After halftime, they won the first five minutes. I had the assignment of Singler; my biggest concern was keeping him off the glass and making him work for everything, but to his credit, he was hitting some tough shots and some were blown defensive assignments on my part. We had everyone pretty much in check and no one else was shooting very well. They were beating us on the glass, they were bringing 6'10's off the bench one after the other, and we were bringing 6'3's off the bench. We were clearly outsized, but we had to counter that with playing hard and making smart, strategic plays. At the end of the day, they just overpowered us with their size; Sheyer and Smith had a good stretch where they scored the majority of their points without working hard for them, like they had been doing throughout a lot of the game. Even though all my shots felt good, they just were not falling; it was bizarre. It was not one of my proudest moments. We were defeated, but I felt like we played our hardest, though it was not enough to advance to the Elite Eight.

Back in the locker room, I don't know how, but I was able to hold back my emotion; Kramer let out some tears; he played his heart out throughout the season. Mark was a strong force for us with unselfish acts of play, giving great plays when he was in and always with a great attitude; a very strong individual with character. We headed back home; the season was over. The questions will start to be asked; who is going to stay and who is leaving?

Chapter 27

Post-season

We held the post-season banquet, where awards were given for Mr. Hustle and Most Valuable Player on the team. Some administrative people gave speeches, Coach Paint gave a few remarks, and at the end, the seniors reflected back on their careers and said whatever they wanted to say about the coaches because, frankly, it didn't matter at this point. E'twaun won Most Valuable Player, which was well deserved. Mark won Mr. Hustle. Mark and Chris made sure that they plugged little jokes here and there about the coaching staff. I just wanted to thank

everyone for the opportunity to play with such an historical program. I let them know that I enjoyed my experience and my time spent at Purdue. The banquet was fun; it was the last time I would be attending one at Purdue seated in a player's seat; it just shows you how fast time flies by.

I didn't take off too much time because it is very easy for me to get out of shape. JaJuan and E'twaun put their names in the draft, but E'twaun had already told me, no matter what, that he would be returning. He just wanted to learn from the process and work out for some teams and see how it all turned out.

Lewis had the surgery on his foot to finally remove the screws and for him to get back to 100% for next year. JaJuan commented he was getting tired of people, around school, and on *Facebook* and *Twitter*. I told him, "It's a grown man's decision and no one else's. Do not make your decision off emotions, make it a wise decision and do what is going to make you happy."

He said, "KG, I want to leave, man, I'm ready to make that step, if they say I am first round, I am gone." I understood. People who were closest to him on the team were telling him that if he stayed, we would be top three in the nation; a potential Final Four team. He said, "Those are all MAYBE'S." They, the media, the fans and the coaches, said the same thing about us this year, and yet we had an injury and did not make it. What happens if the same thing happens next year? Then it is the same situation. There are lots of unknowns that can happen, which is why I told him he had to make the decision for himself. JaJuan had to make the decision alone if he was going to stay in the draft

or go back to school. He had two workouts; the first one was with the Boston Celtics. He said that he did well and was talking to Danny Ainge, who told him that he needed to go back to school and pick up weight. He said, "You don't even need to put up big numbers as long as you pick up weight, then you would be fine." JaJuan was tormented and was telling me, "If I haven't picked up the weight in three years, I should stay out, hire a chef and a trainer who is focused on only me to make sure that I pick up the weight that I need to pick up."

This was Wednesday of the week that he needed to make the decision. This was one of the reasons that made it so difficult. He knew there would be chances that he could go second round, and he was willing to live with the choice. He said to me, "I just want to play basketball."

He went to the Rockets for the next workout, and they pretty much said the same thing as the Celtics. So it came down to the workouts. As of that Wednesday, in spite of what was told to him from Danny Ainge, he remained in the draft, but from the sound of his voice, you could tell that he was swaying the other direction and questioning himself concerning whether it was wise to go back to school. He said the only real thing that was making him think of returning were his teammates. He said that Rob left him a long text message expressing his input, basically saying if he were a guaranteed first round pick, then he would advise him say stay in the draft, but with the chance of going second round and with the money not being guaranteed, he should come back and strive for a Final Four again. Rob's words were, "We came in together, and we leave together." JaJuan said that Rob made a lot of sense and helped him put things in perspective. The day that he had to make the decision, we drove back to Purdue from Indianapolis. He disclosed me the night before what he was going to do. He was excited about the NBA, but in my mind, as his friend, I'm glad that he went back to school. He can make more money next year and afterwards, and he will not regret his last season. Now that he is coming back, all I can say now is, "Big Ten and the country look out for JaJuan Johnson, best big man in the nation."

E'twaun said he wanted to experience the process and learn from the experience. He was always determined to come back. To me, I still think E'twaun is an underrated, great guard in the nation. He led our team in scoring all three years and his recognition seems to not be mentioned on the level it deserves.

I graduated on May 15th; my family was so proud. I was the first person in my family to graduate from a major university. As soon I received my diploma, I took it outside of the commencement and my mom made sure that it was in her hands so that it would make it back to Florida with her so she could show it off.

Boiler

up!!!

Biography

My name is Keaton Leonard Grant. I was born in Winter Haven, Florida to James and Celia Grant. I am the younger of two sons; my older brother's name is James. I was raised in Kissimmee, FL, where I graduated from Gateway High School in 2005. After high school, I decided to attend prep school at Bridgton Academy in Maine. I attended Bridgton Academy for one year as a postgraduate. After finishing my first year at Bridgton, I then decided to attend Purdue University. I graduated in 2010 with a Bachelors of Science. During my career at Purdue, I played four years on the men's basketball team, later becoming the player with the most wins in the university's history. Aside from basketball, I am pursuing a career in the entrepreneurial field, hoping one day to start a variety of businesses. I also plan to start a foundation to encourage youth to perform to the best of their abilities.

As a young boy and with some of my first memories, I immediately became interested in sports, particularly playing football, baseball and basketball. I decided to stop playing baseball at an early age because I felt that it was not exciting enough for me. I later stopped playing football as well. My brother played but tore his ACL in high school playing football, and from this experience I decided that if I did take the risk of getting hurt, it would be for the sport that I *loved* most, which was basketball. I gained an interest in basketball in the eighth grade. Discouragement from administrators at my middle school spurred me to play to my full potential, even though they often said that I would not perform well enough to play varsity basketball as a freshman. Some even said that my dreams of playing college basketball were near impossible. I remember the sarcastic laughing. At this point, I made up in my mind that I would never quit nor let anyone limit my possibilities.

Out of high school, I originally committed to attend the University of Missouri. Quinn Snyder was the head coach at that time. I later learned that I missed the school's qualifying ACT score by a single point. I then decided to attend prep school. After which, I reopened my recruitment for other schools.

My basketball career at Purdue was eventful. I was named team MVP my sophomore year. As a team, we made it to the NCAA tournament four straight years and made two Sweet Sixteen appearances. More accomplishments as a team were a Big Ten regular season championship and one tournament Big Ten championship.

Thank You's:

I want to thank God first and foremost; without Him none of this is possible.

Extra thank you to My family, Keith and Allison Edmonds: for believing in me and always supporting and being my backbone, especially my brother who is my right hand and is always keeping me on track and being there when I needed him the most.

To all my teammates and their families: you were like brothers to me and made my experience a wonderful experience; we had each other's backs through the thick and thin.

To especially E'twaun, JJ, Lewis, and Rob: we have been through a lot and will always cherish the experience that we all had; a lot of laughs and a lot of success.

To all four of their families: who have looked after me like I was kin to them throughout the years; whether it was a place to stay or food on the holidays and always giving encouraging words. These times will never be forgotten.

To the coaches: for believing in me and giving me the opportunity to play for such a great program. Also for helping mold me into a solid basketball player. You are one-of-kind coaches, and I know a national championship is coming soon.

To Mrs. Lyn: for being a mother-like figure. Always looking out for me in tough times and helping me with school work or matters that she did not have to assist with, but decided to do so out of the kindness of her heart; I will never forget what she has done for me and how she helped me through the years.

To Tony Gaskins: who has been a guide for me and gave me encouraging words and any advice when I needed it.

To my church family in the Florida: who has kept me in their prayers and kept in touch with me even though I was in Indiana.

A **BIG** shout out to the Paint Crew: who have cheered me on during my four years and who have made the experience such a memorable one for me.

To Dan Washington and Doug Schwartz: who have been mentors to me, and have shown me different things about business. Thanks for helping and looking out for me throughout the years since my family was so far away.

Ron Whitaker: for the support he has shown throughout the years and going out of his way to lend a helping hand when he did not have to do so.

Ed Kennedy: who as a friend, has always kept it honest with me, showing the love and support that he has shown the team and me through many of years going on the road or being in the Mackey arena.

The whole Purdue Alumni Association, including the John Purdue Club. Without them most things would not be possible. Thanks for believing in the program and providing us with financial support, which makes it all possible.

To Sterling Blake: who has helped me in many ways from just mentoring me as a person and giving encouraging words when needed.

Up and Coming:

The Keaton Grant Foundation's mission is to provide substantial resources that will enable youth for college in areas of mentorship, tutoring, sponsorship and scholarship.

Stix & Stonez clothing/Diamonds & Pearls

Websites

Keatongrant.com

Keatongrantincorporated.org

Keatongrantfoundation.org

Stixandstonezclothing.com

Contacts

Kgrant.inc@gmail.com

Twitter.com/kgrant5

Made in the USA
Charleston, SC
03 January 2011